Your Credit Score

How to Fix, Improve, and Protect the 3-Digit Number that Shapes Your Financial Future

Liz Pulliam Weston

PEARSON
Prentice
Hall

An Imprint of PEARSON EDUCATION

Upper Saddle River, NJ • New York • London
San Francisco • Toronto • Sydney • Tokyo • Singapore
Hong Kong • Cape Town • Madrid • Paris • Milan
Munich • Amsterdam

www.ft-ph.com

Library of Congress Publication in Data: 2004109280

Publisher: *Tim Moore*
Executive Editor: *Jim Boyd*
Editorial Assistant: *Richard Winkler*
Development Editor: *Russ Hall*
Marketing Manager: *Martin Litkowski*
International Marketing Manager: *Tim Galligan*
Cover Designer: *Sandra Schroeder*
Managing Editor: *Gina Kanouse*
Project Editor: *Christy Hackerd*
Copy Editor: *Karen Gill*
Senior Indexer: *Cheryl Lenser*
Interior Designer: *Gloria Schurick*
Compositor: *Gloria Schurick and Tolman Creek Design*
Manufacturing Buyer: *Dan Uhrig*

Prentice Hall offers excellent discounts on this book when ordered in quantity for bulk purchases or special sales. For more information, please contact U.S. Corporate and Government Sales, 1-800-382-3419, corpsales@pearsontechgroup.com. For sales outside the U.S., please contact International Sales, international@pearsontechgroup.com.

Printed in the United States of America

Fourth Printing
10 9 8 7 6 5 4

ISBN 0-13-148603-9

Pearson Education LTD.
Pearson Education Australia PTY, Limited.
Pearson Education Singapore, Pte. Ltd.
Pearson Education North Asia, Ltd.
Pearson Education Canada, Ltd.
Pearson Educatión de Mexico, S.A. de C.V.
Pearson Education—Japan
Pearson Education Malaysia, Pte. Ltd.

Your Credit Score

How to Fix, Improve, and Protect the 3-Digit Number
that Shapes Your Financial Future

To Will

Contents

Acknowledgments

Credit and credit scoring can be a mysterious, complex subject, which means any journalist trying to cover this area of personal finance needs great sources. I've been extraordinarily fortunate to have found experts who not only knew their fields but who were willing to spend time helping me understand them, too.

At the top of this list is Craig Watts, spokesman for Fair Isaac Corp., who invested hours researching and carefully answering my endless questions. Several of his colleagues at the company were also generous with their time and expertise, including Ryan Sjobald and Lamont Boyd.

Allen Bond, Ginny Ferguson, and Don Scott were among the many mortgage professionals who helped me learn about the home lending game, returning my calls even as their own phones rang off the hook during the refinance boom. My credit card and insurance sources are likewise too numerous to list, but special thanks to Gerri Detweiler of UltimateCredit.com, Robert McKinley of CardWeb, Robert Hunter of the Consumer Federation of America, Gail Hillebrand at Consumers Union, Deanne Loonin and Robin Leonard at Nolo Press, and the folks at Insurance Information Institute, VISA, and Citibank. Thanks, too, to Beth Givens of the Privacy Rights Clearinghouse and Linda Foley of the Identity Theft Resource Center for their insights into credit fraud.

Sam Gerdano of the American Bankruptcy Institute and Harvard professor Elizabeth Warren, author of "The Two-Income Trap: Why Middle Class Mothers and Fathers are Going Broke," provided their vast knowledge and perspective about the bankruptcy epidemic in America.

Then there are the cheerleaders—the people who encouraged me to take on and complete this sometimes daunting project. Leading the charge was my husband, Will Weston, who picked up a lot of slack around the house and encouraged me to return to my computer on those many nights when I would have much rather watched a rerun of *Friends*.

My friend and colleague, Kathy Kristof, gave a realistic assessment of what was in store when juggling family, full-time work, and book writing—but told me to go for it anyway.

My editor, Jim Boyd, instantly understood why this book needed to be written and guided me expertly along its route to completion. He and his staff at Pearson Prentice Hall have been terrific.

Finally, I'd like to thank my readers who generously shared their experiences, opinions, praise, and criticism. Your letters and emails helped shape the information in this book and inspired me to keep digging for answers that could make a real difference in your lives.

About the Author

Liz Pulliam Weston is a personal finance columnist whose twice-weekly columns for MSN Money reach more than six million people each month. She's also the author of the question-and-answer column *Money Talk*, which appears in the *Los Angeles Times* and other newspapers throughout the country. Weston is a weekly guest on CNBC's *Power Lunch* and has appeared on NBC, Fine Living, PAX TV, and other networks.

Formerly a personal finance writer for the *Times*, Weston has won numerous reporting awards. She was part of a three-member writing team that won a Gerald Loeb Award for coverage of the Comparator Systems penny stock scandal in 1997. She also was a member of the *Anchorage Daily News* team that won a Pulitzer Prize for Meritorious Public Service in 1989 for coverage of the alcoholism epidemic among native Alaskans.

Weston is a graduate of the certified financial planner training program at University of California, Irvine. She lives in Los Angeles with her husband and daughter.

1

WHY YOUR CREDIT SCORE MATTERS

In recent years, a simple three-digit number has become critical to your financial life.

This number, known as a credit score, is designed to predict the possibility that you won't pay your bills. Credit scores are handy for lenders, but they can have enormous repercussions for your wallet, your future, and your peace of mind.

How Your Credit Score Affects You

If your credit score is high enough, you'll qualify for a lender's best rates and terms. Your mailbox will be stuffed with low-rate offers from credit card issuers, and mortgage lenders will fight for your business. You'll get great deals on auto financing if you need a car, home loans if you want to buy or improve a house, and small business loans if you decide to start a new venture.

If your score is low or nonexistent, however, you'll enter a no-man's-land where mainstream credit is all but impossible to come by. If you find someone to lend you money, you'll pay high rates and fat fees for the privilege. A bad or even mediocre credit score easily can cost you tens of thousands and even hundreds of thousands of dollars in your lifetime.

You don't even have to have tons of credit problems to pay a price. Sometimes all it takes is a single missed payment to knock more than 100 points off your credit score and put you in a lender's high-risk category.

That would be scary enough if we were just talking about loans. But landlords and insurance companies also use credit scores to evaluate applicants. A good score can win you cheaper premiums and better apartments; a bad score can make insurance more expensive and a place to live hard to find.

Yet too many people know far too little about credit scores and how they work. Here's just a sample of the kinds of emails and letters I get every day from people puzzling over their credit:[1]

"I just closed all of my credit card accounts trying to improve my credit. Now I hear that closing accounts can actually hurt my score. How can I recover from this? Should I try to reopen accounts so that I can have a higher amount of available credit?" Hallie in Shreveport, LA

"How do you get credit if you don't have it? I keep getting turned down, and the reason is always 'insufficient credit history.' How can I get a decent credit score if I don't have credit?" Manuel in San Diego, CA

"I am a 25-year-old male who made a few bad credit decisions while in college, as many of us do. I need to improve my credit drastically so I do not continue to get my eyes poked out on interest. What can I do to boost my credit score fast?" Stephen in Dallas, TX

"I joined a credit counseling program because I was in way over my head. But my wife and I plan on buying a house within the next three years, and she has expressed concern that my participation in this debt management program could hurt my credit score. What should I do to help my overall chances with the mortgage process and get the best rate possible?" Paul in Lodi, NJ

"I'm 33 and have never had a single late payment or credit issue in my life. Yet, my credit score isn't as high as I thought it would be. What does it take to get a perfect score?" Brian in South Bend, IN

---

1 As with other real-life anecdotes in this book, the writers' anonymity has been protected and their messages might have been edited for clarity.

What these readers sense, and what credit experts know, is that ignorance about your credit score can cost you. Sometimes people with great scores get offered lousy loan deals but don't realize they can qualify for better terms. More often, people with bad or mediocre credit get all the loans they want, but they don't realize the high price they're paying.

What It Costs Long Term to Have a Poor or Mediocre Credit Score

If you need an example of exactly how much a credit score can matter, let's examine how these numbers affect two friends, Emily and Karen.

Both women got their first credit card in college and carried an $8,000 balance on average over the years. (Carrying a balance isn't smart financially, but unfortunately, it's an ingrained habit with many credit card users.)

Emily and Karen also bought new cars after graduation, financing their purchases with $20,000 auto loans. Every seven years, they replaced their existing cars with new ones until they bought their last vehicles at age 70.

Each bought her first home with $350,000 mortgages at age 30, and then moved up to a larger house with $450,000 mortgages after turning 40.

Neither has ever suffered the embarrassment of being rejected for a loan or turned down for a credit card.

But here the similarities end.

Emily was always careful to pay her bills on time, all the time, and typically paid more than the minimum balance owed. Lenders responded to her responsible use of credit by offering her more credit cards at good rates and terms. They also tended to increase her credit limits regularly. That allowed Emily to spread her credit card balance across several cards. All these factors helped give Emily an excellent credit score. Whenever a lender tried to raise her interest rate, she would politely threaten to transfer her balance to another card. As a result, Emily's average interest rate on her cards was 9.9 percent.

Karen, by contrast, didn't always pay on time, frequently paid only the minimum due, and tended to max out the cards that she had. That made lenders reluctant to increase her credit limits or offer her new cards. Although the two women owed the same amount on average, Karen tended to carry larger balances on fewer cards. All these factors hurt Karen's credit—not enough to prevent her from getting loans, but enough for lenders to charge her more. Karen had much less negotiating power when it came to interest rates. Her average interest rate on her credit cards was 19.9 percent.

Credit Cards

	Emily	Karen
Credit score	750	650
Interest rate	9.90%	19.90%
Annual interest costs	$792	$1,592
Lifetime interest paid	$39,600	$79,600
Karen's penalty		$40,000

Emily's careful credit use paid off with her first car loan. She got the best available rate, and she continued to do so every time she bought a new car until her last purchase at age 70. Thanks to her lower credit score, Karen's rate was three percentage points higher.

Auto Loans

	Emily	Karen
Credit score	750	650
Interest rate	5.00%	8.00%
Monthly payment	$377	$406
Interest cost per loan	$2,646	$4,332
Lifetime interest paid	$21,166	$34,653
Karen's penalty		$13,487

The differences continued when the women bought their houses. During the 10 years that the women owned their first homes, Emily paid $68,000 less in interest.

Mortgage 1 ($350,000)

	Emily	Karen
Credit score	750	650
Interest rate	5.50%	7.375%
Monthly payment	$1,987	$2,417
Total interest paid (10 years)	$174,760	$243,020
Karen's penalty		$68,261

Karen's interest penalty only grew when the two women moved up to larger houses. Over the 30-year life of their mortgages, Karen paid nearly $200,000 more in interest.

Mortgage 2 ($200,000)

	Emily	Karen
Credit score	750	650
Interest rate	5.50%	7.375%
Monthly payment	$2,555	$3,108
Total interest paid (30 years)	$469,818	$668,894
Karen's penalty		$199,894

Karen's total lifetime penalty for less-than-stellar credit? More than $320,000.

If anything, these examples underestimate the true financial cost of mediocre credit:

- The interest rates in the examples date from early 2004—a time when rates were near record lows. Higher prevailing interest rates would increase the penalty Karen pays.

- Karen probably paid insurance premiums that were 20 percent to 30 percent higher than Emily's, and she might have had more trouble finding an apartment, all because of her credit.

- The examples don't count "opportunity cost"—what Karen could have achieved financially if she weren't paying so much more interest.

Because more of Karen's paycheck went to lenders, she had less money available for other goals: vacations, a second home, college educations for her kids, and retirement.

In fact, if Karen had been able to invest the extra money she paid in interest instead of sending it to banks and credit card companies, her savings might have grown by a whopping $2 million by the time she was 70.

With so much less disposable income and financial security, you wouldn't be surprised if Karen also experienced more anxiety about money. Financial problems can take their toll in innumerable ways, from stress-related illnesses to marital problems and divorce.

So, if you've ever wondered why some families struggle while others in the same economic bracket seem to do just fine, the answers typically lie with their financial habits—including how they handle credit.

How Credit Scoring Came into Being

The question remains: How did one little number come to have such an outsized effect on our lives?

Credit scoring has been in widespread use by lenders for several decades. By the end of the 1970s, most major lenders used some kind of credit-scoring formulas to decide whether to accept or reject applications.

Many were introduced to credit scoring by two pioneers in the field: engineer Bill Fair and mathematician Earl Isaac, who founded the firm Fair Isaac in 1956. Over the years, the pair convinced lenders that mathematical formulas could do a better job of predicting whether an applicant would default than even the most experienced loan officers.

A formula wasn't as subject to human whims and biases. It wouldn't turn down a potentially good credit risk because the applicant was the "wrong" race, religion, or gender, and it wouldn't accept a bad risk because the applicant was a friend.

Credit scoring, aided by ever more powerful computers, was also fast. Lending decisions could be made in a matter of minutes, rather than days or weeks.

Early on, each company had its own credit-scoring formula, tailored to the amount of risk it wanted to take, its history with various types of borrowers, and the kind of people it attracted as customers. The factors that fed into the formula varied, but many took into account the applicant's income, occupation, length of time with an employer, length of time at an address, and some of the information available on his or her credit report, such as the longest time that a payment was ever overdue.

These calculations took place behind the scenes, invisible to the consumer and understood by a relatively small number of experts and loan executives.

The cost to develop and implement these custom formulas was—and still is—considerable. It was not unusual to spend $100,000 or more and take 12 months just to set one up. In addition, not every creditor had a big enough database to work with, especially if the company wanted to branch out into a new line of lending. A credit card lender that wanted to start offering car loans, for example, might find that its database couldn't adequately predict risk in vehicle lending.

That led to credit scores that are based on the biggest lending databases of all—those that are held at the major credit bureaus, which include Equifax, Experian, and TransUnion. Fair Isaac developed the first credit bureau-based scoring system in the mid-1980s, and the idea quickly caught on.

Instead of basing their calculations on any single lender's experience, this type of scoring factored in the behavior of literally millions of borrowers. The model looked for patterns of behavior that indicated a borrower might default, as well as patterns that indicated a borrower was likely to pay as agreed. The score evaluated the consumer's history of paying bills, the number and type of credit accounts, how much available credit the customer was using, and other factors.

This credit-scoring model was useful for more than just accepting or rejecting applicants. Some lenders decided to accept higher-risk clients but to charge them more to compensate for the greater chance that they might default. Lenders also used scores to screen vast numbers of borrowers to find potential future customers. Instead of waiting for people to apply, credit card companies and other lenders could send out reams of preapproved offers to likely prospects.

How Credit Use Has Changed Over the Years

Credit scoring is one of the reasons why consumer credit absolutely exploded in the 1990s. Lenders felt more confident about making loans to wider groups of people because they had a more precise tool for measuring risk. Credit scoring also allowed them to make decisions faster, enabling them to make more loans. The result was an unprecedented rise in the amount of available consumer credit. Here are just a few examples of how available credit expanded during that time:

- The total volume of consumer loans—credit cards, auto loans, and other non mortgage debt—more than doubled between 1990 and 2000, to $1.7 trillion.

- The amount of credit card debt outstanding rose nearly three-fold between 1990 and 2002, from $173 billion to $661 billion.

- Home equity lending soared from $261 billion in 1993 to more than $1 trillion 10 years later.

Credit scoring got a huge boost in 1995. That's when the country's two biggest mortgage-finance agencies, Fannie Mae and Freddie Mac, recommended lenders use FICO credit scores. Because Fannie Mae and

Freddie Mac purchase more than two-thirds of the mortgages made, their recommendations carry enormous weight in the home loan industry.

The recommendations are also what finally began to bring credit scoring to the public's attention.

If you've ever applied for a mortgage, you know it's a much more involved process than getting a credit card. When you apply for a Visa or MasterCard, you typically fill out a relatively brief form, submit it, and get your answer back in a few days or weeks by mail. In other words, there isn't much personal contact.

Contrast that with a mortgage. Not only do you have to provide a lot more information about your finances, but getting a home loan requires that you have ongoing personal contact with a loan officer or mortgage broker. You might be asked to clarify something in your application, be told to supply more information, or be given updates on how your request for funds was being received.

Consumer's Fight for Truth About Credit Scores

It was in the course of those conversations that an increasing number of consumers starting hearing about FICOs and credit scores. For the first time, people learned that the reason they did or didn't get the loan they wanted was because of a three-digit number. It became obvious that lenders were putting a lot of stock in these mysterious scores.

But when consumers tried asking for more details, they often hit a brick wall. Fair Isaac, the leader in the credit-scoring world, wanted to keep the information secret. The company said it worried that consumers wouldn't understand the nuances of credit scoring, or they would try to "game the system" if they knew more. Fair Isaac feared that its formulas would lose their predictive ability if consumers started changing their behavior to boost their scores.

Now, some sympathetic mortgage officials didn't buy into Fair Isaac's company line. They thought consumers deserved to know their score, and these officials also often tried to explain how the numbers were created.

Unfortunately, because Fair Isaac wouldn't disclose the formula details, a lot of these explanations were dead wrong. Even more unfortunately, some loan officers perpetuate these myths about credit scoring, despite the fact that we have much more information about what goes into them. (You'll read more on these myths in Chapter 4, "Credit Scoring Myths.")

Resentment about the secret nature of credit scores came to a head in early 2000. That's when one of the then-new breed of Internet lenders, E-Loan, defied Fair Isaac by letting consumers view their FICO credit scores. For about a month, people could actually take a peak at their scores online and learn some rudimentary information about what the numbers meant. Some 25,000 consumers took advantage of the free service before E-Loan's source for credit-scoring information was cut off.

But the proverbial cat was out of the bag. A few months later, with consumer advocates demanding disclosure and lawmakers drafting legislation requiring it, Fair Isaac caved. It posted the 22 factors affecting a credit score on its Web site, grouped into the five categories you'll read about in the next chapter. Shortly after that, the company partnered with credit bureau Equifax to provide consumers with their credit scores and reports for a $12.95 fee.

In late 2003, Congress finally got around to passing a law that gave people a right to see their scores. By the time this update to the Fair Credit Reporting Act was signed into law, though, access to credit scores was almost old hat.

Credit Controversies

Controversies over credit scoring continue to rage. Here are just of few of them.

Credit Scoring's Vulnerability to Errors

No matter how good the mathematics of credit scoring, it's based on information in your credit report—which may be, and frequently is, wrong. Sometimes the errors are small or irrelevant, such as when your credit file lists a past employer as a current employer. Other times the problems are significant, such as when your file contains accounts that don't belong to you. Many people only discover this misinformation after they've been turned down for credit.

The credit bureaus handle billions of pieces of data every day, so to some extent, errors, outdated, and missing information are inevitable—but the credit-reporting system often makes it difficult to get rid of errors after you spot them.

The problem is only getting worse. The rise in automated lending decisions means a human might never see your application or notice that something's awry. The explosion in identity theft, with its 10 million victims a year, means more bad, fraudulent information is included in innocent people's credit files every day.

Patricia of Seattle, Washington, tells of the ongoing horror of becoming a victim:

"I've always been careful about protecting my identity. Unfortunately, when I was trying to purchase a home, the real estate broker, to whom I'd given my application with birth date and Social Security number, had her laptop stolen. My worst fears came true when, four months later, I suddenly had creditors calling me like crazy asking why I wasn't paying on accounts that were just recently opened in my name. On top of this, I learned the criminals had also stolen my mail with preapproved credit cards. This has created a nightmare of time, work, and frustration trying to clean up my credit history. It's been over two years now, and I'm still working with the major credit-reporting agencies as we speak."

Credit Scoring's Complexity

You're being judged by the formula, so shouldn't it be easy to understand and predictable? Not even credit-scoring experts can always forecast in advance how certain behaviors will affect a score. Because the formula takes into account so many variables, the best answer they can muster is: "It depends."

The variety of different scoring formulas and different approaches among lenders can confuse matters even further.

Lenders can get scores calculated from different versions of the FICO formula. They also can have in-house formulas that incorporate a FICO score along with other information that might punish or reward certain behaviors more heavily than the FICO formula does on its own. Some call the result a FICO score, even though that's not technically correct.

Not surprisingly, this causes confusion for consumers and mortgage professionals alike.

A.J. Cleland, an Indianapolis mortgage broker, discovered how different scores can be when trying to help a client who had been turned down for a loan by a bank. The bank reported the client's FICO score was 602, whereas the FICO score Cleland pulled for the client—on the same day and from the same credit bureau—was 31 points lower.

"I called my credit provider and was informed that there are different types of reports and different scores," Cleland said. "I thought your score was your score, period."

Credit Scoring's Use for Noncredit Decisions

I mentioned earlier that your landlord or employer might check your credit and your credit score in evaluating your application; however, the most controversial noncredit use of scoring is in insurance.

Insurers have discovered that there's an enormously strong link between the quality of your credit and the likelihood you'll file a claim. They can't really explain it, but every large study of the issue has confirmed that this link exists. The worse your credit, the more likely you will cost an insurer money. The better your credit, the less likely you are to have an accident or otherwise suffer an insured loss.

As a result, more than 90 percent of homeowners and auto insurers use credit scoring to decide who to cover and what premiums to charge them.

That outrages many consumers and consumer advocates who don't see a logical connection between credit and insurance. Julie, a city worker in Poulsbo, Washington, saw her insurances soar after a divorce and subsequent bankruptcy trashed her credit.[2]

"I have had the same insurer for 30 years, never been late, never missed a payment, never had an accident, and never filed a claim—yet now I pay the price of higher rates. I absolutely do not understand how this is fair."

This leads to the final controversy, spelled out in the next section.

Credit Scoring's Potential Unfairness

Developers of credit scoring point out their formulas are designed not to discriminate. Credit scores don't factor in your income, race, religion, ethnic background, or anything else that's not on your credit report.

But it's not clear if the result of those formulas actually is nondiscriminatory. Some consumer advocates worry that some disadvantaged groups might suffer disproportionately as a result of credit scoring.

Among their theories: People who have low incomes or who live in some minority neighborhoods might have less access to mainstream lenders and thus have worse credit scores. The lenders these disadvantaged populations do use—finance companies, subprime lenders, and community groups—might not report to credit bureaus, making it harder to build a credit history. If these

---

2   Like many divorced people, Julie discovered that her ex still had the power to trash her credit long after the marriage was over. His unpaid bills, run up on once-joint accounts, showed up on her credit report and ultimately led her to file bankruptcy.

lenders do report to the bureaus, their accounts might count for less in the credit-scoring formula than those of mainstream lenders. Seasonal work is also more prevalent in some neighborhoods, which can lead to a higher rate of late payments in the off-seasons.

Even if credit scoring doesn't discriminate against groups, it might discriminate against you.

No credit-scoring system is perfect. Lenders know that their formulas will reject a certain number of people who actually would have paid their bills. Another group will be accepted as good risks, but then default.

If these groups get too large, the lender has trouble. When too many bad applicants are accepted, the lender's profits plunge. When too many good applicants are rejected, the lender's competitors can scoop them up and make more money.

But lenders accept a certain number of misclassified applicants as a cost of doing business.

That's little comfort to you, if you're one of the responsible ones who loses out on the mortgage you need to buy a home, or if you end up paying more for it.

Conclusion

Given all the problems with credit scoring, it's understandable that some people think the system is fatally flawed. Some of my readers tell me they're so angry about scoring and the behavior of lenders in general that they've cut up their credit cards and are determined to live a credit-free life.

The rest of us, though, live in a world where credit is all but a necessity. Few of us can pay cash for a home, and many need loans to buy cars. Credit can help launch a new business or pay for an education. And most Americans like the convenience of using credit cards. Although it's true that improper use of credit can be disastrous, credit properly used can enhance your life.

If we want to have credit, we need to know about how credit scoring works. Knowledge is power, and the tools I'll give you in this book will help you take control of your credit and your financial life.

2

HOW CREDIT SCORING
WORKS

The first thing you need to know about your credit score is that you don't have *a* credit score: you have many, and they change all the time.

Credit scores are designed to be a snapshot of your credit picture—typically, the picture that's contained in your credit report. New information is constantly being added to your report, and old information is being deleted. Those changes affect your score.

That can be good news or bad news. The good news is that if you have a bad score now, you're not stuck with it forever. You can do a lot to improve your situation and make yourself more credit-worthy in lenders' eyes.

The bad news is that you can't rest on your laurels. When you have a good score, you need to constantly monitor your credit to make sure it stays that way.

You also should know that there's more than one credit-scoring system out there. In fact, there are currently more than 100 credit-scoring models being marketed to lenders. The best-known credit-scoring model, the FICO, is designed to predict whether a borrower will default. But credit-scoring systems have been created to do all of the following:

- Detect fraud in credit or insurance applications

- Calculate the amount of profit a credit card issuer is likely to make on a particular account

- Predict the risk of a specific kind of default, such a bankruptcy

- Forecast the probability that a policyholder will cost an insurer money

- Anticipate the risk that a consumer will default on a certain type of account, such as an auto loan, a mortgage, a cellular phone account, or a utility bill

- Estimate how much a borrower is likely to pay, if anything, on a delinquent account

- Anticipate which customers might close a credit card account or pay the balance down to zero

- Predict the likelihood that someone will respond to a direct-mail credit card solicitation

The vast majority of these scoring systems are developed by the same company that created the FICO: Fair Isaac. In addition, the credit bureaus and some outside companies have created their own formulas.

All that being said, you're far more likely to be affected by a FICO score or its cousin, the NextGen score, than any other type of credit score. FICO is the industry leader. It's used in literally billions of lending decisions each year, including 75 percent of mortgage-lending assessments.

That's why the information in this chapter and elsewhere is based on how the FICO formula calculates your score. Other formula designs might differ somewhat in their details, but the behaviors that help and hurt your score are pretty consistent across the various systems.

Here are some other facts about credit scoring that you should keep in mind:

- **You need to have and use credit to have a credit score**—
  The classic and NextGen FICO formulas need at least one account on your credit report that have been open for six months and one account that's been updated in the past six months (it can be the same account). If your credit history is too thin, or you've stopped using credit for a period of time, there might not be enough current data in your file to create a regular credit score. (That doesn't mean you can't be "scored." In mid-2004, Fair Isaac introduced the FICO Expansion Score for lenders who want to evaluate people with thin or nonexistent credit histories. This new score uses nontraditional information sources like payday lenders and companies that monitor bounced checks.)

- **A credit score usually isn't the only thing lenders consider**—In mortgage lending decisions, in particular, lenders weigh a lot of other information, including your employment history and stability, the value of the property you're buying or refinancing, your income and your total monthly debt payments as a percentage of that income, among other factors.

  So, although credit scores can be a powerful force in lending decisions, they might not be the sole determinant of whether you get credit.

- **Credit-scoring systems were designed for lenders, not consumers**—In other words, scores weren't created to be easy to understand. The actual formulas, and many of the details of how they work, are closely guarded trade secrets.

The credit-scoring companies don't want the process to be transparent or predictable, as discussed in the previous chapter. They fear that letting out too many details would allow competitors to copy their formulas. They also worry that their formulas would lose their ability to predict risk if consumers knew exactly how to beat them.

We know more about the formulas than ever before, and certainly enough for you to improve your score. But given the number of variables involved and the mystery still surrounding credit scoring, you won't be able to forecast exactly how every action will affect a score, or how quickly.

What Is a Good Score?

One of the first questions many people have about credit scoring is what score lenders consider "good." There is, however, no single answer to that question.

Generally, of course, the higher the score, the better. Each lender makes its own decision about where to draw the line, based on how much risk it wants to take and how much profit it thinks it can make with a given blend of customers. Many lenders don't have a single cut-off but may have many, with each segment qualifying for different rates and terms. Finally, as noted earlier, a credit score is usually only one factor in the lending decision. Although scores typically have a big influence, a lender might decide that other factors are more important.

You can see from this national distribution chart of FICO credit scores that most of the U.S. population has a FICO score of 700 or higher. Many lenders use 700 or 720 as the cutoff for giving borrowers their best rates and terms. Many also use 620 as a cut-off point. Companies that deal with borrowers below that level are often called "subprime" lenders, because their riskier borrowers are considered less than "prime."

FICO Credit Score	Percent with Score
300–499	1%
500–549	5%
550–599	7%
600–649	11%
650–699	16%
700–749	20%
750–799	29%
800–850	11%

The company that creates the FICO is now marketing an updated version called the NextGen. The NextGen has a wider possible score range: instead of 300 to 850, the lowest possible score is 150 and the highest is 950. Your actual score, though, predicts about the same amount of risk in both systems. So, a 750 is considered a low-risk score under both the FICO and NextGen formulas.

Your Credit Report: The Building Blocks for Your Score

Because your score is constructed from the information in your credit report, it's worth looking at what you'll find there.

In addition to identifying information about you—your name, address, and Social Security number—your report lists the following:

- **Your credit accounts**—Sometimes called "trade lines," these include loans, credit cards, and other credit accounts you've opened. Your report lists the type of account, how long ago you opened it, your balances, and details of your payment history.

- **Requests for your credit**—These are known as "inquiries," and there are basically two kinds. When you apply for credit, you authorize the lender to view your credit history. This is known as a "hard inquiry" and can affect your credit score. You might also see inquiries that you didn't initiate. These "soft inquiries" are typically made when a lender orders your credit report to make you a preapproved credit offer. Such marketing efforts don't affect your score.

- **Public records and collections**—These can include collection accounts, bankruptcies, tax liens, foreclosures, wage garnishments, lawsuits, and judgments.

Public records are culled from state and county courthouses. Lenders or collection agencies report most of the other information in your report.

This data is collected, stored, and updated by credit bureaus, which are private, for-profit companies. The three major credit bureaus are Equifax, Experian (formerly known as TRW), and Trans Union, and their business is selling information about you to lenders.

Because they're competitors, the bureaus typically don't share information, and not all lenders report information to all three bureaus. In fact, if you get copies of your credit reports from the bureaus on the same day, you're likely to notice at least a few differences among them. An account that's listed on one credit bureau's report might not show up on the others, for example, or the balances showing on your various accounts might differ from bureau to bureau.

Because your score is based on the information that's in your report at a given credit bureau, the number differs depending on which bureau's credit report is used.

Also, each time you or a lender "pulls" your score (in other words, orders a score to be calculated), it's likely to be at least somewhat different, because the information on which it's based probably has changed. Fair Isaac says most people's scores don't change all that much in a short period, but about 25 percent of consumers can expect to see their scores at a single bureau vary by more than 20 points over a three-month stretch.

There also are time limits to what can appear on your credit report. Although positive information can appear indefinitely, negative marks—late payments, collection actions, and foreclosures—by federal law generally must be removed after seven years. Bankruptcies can be reported for 10 years. Inquiries should be deleted in two years.

How Your Score Is Calculated

When most of us think of scores, we think of the relatively straightforward systems used in sports or in school tests. You get points (and possibly demerits) for certain actions, behaviors, or answers, and those are totaled to determine your score.

Credit scoring isn't nearly so easy. Credit-scoring models use "multivariate" formulas. That basically means that the value of any given bit of information in your report might depend on other bits of information.

To understand how this works, let's use a noncredit example. Say that your sister calls you to report that her husband is more than an hour late in coming home from work, and she asks if you think he's having an affair. To answer the question, you would need to review what you know about this man, including his attitude about his family, his general moral standards, and whether he's had dalliances in the past. Using all these variables, you could try to predict whether your brother-in-law is likely to be stepping out—or might just have stopped off to buy his wife an anniversary present.

Let's suppose that your brother-in-law is a stand-up guy. But you've personally observed your neighbor in a clinch with a woman who was not his wife. If your neighbor was an hour late in coming home and *his* wife asked you your opinion of his likely faithfulness, you might reach quite a different conclusion. So the same behavior—coming home late—could evoke two very different predictions based on the information at your disposal.

The number of factors that the FICO formulas evaluate is infinitely greater, so you can see how difficult it can be sometimes to predict the outcomes of certain behaviors.

There's one thing that's always true, though: The FICO model is set up to place more value on current behavior than on past behavior. That means that the effect of your old credit troubles lessens over time if you start handling credit more responsibly.

However, the scores are also designed to react strongly to any signs that a once-good risk might be turning bad. That's why someone with a good score might suffer more heavily from a late payment.

It's generally a lot easier to lose points on your score than it is to gain them back, which is why it's so important to know how to improve and protect your score.

The Five Most Important Factors

Now that you understand in general how credit scores are calculated, we can move on to some specifics. The following are the five main factors that affect your score according to their relative level of importance, along with a percentage figure that reflects how heavily that factor is weighed in calculating FICO scores for the general population. Each factor might weigh more or less heavily in your individual score, depending on your credit situation.

Your Payment History

This makes up about 35 percent of the typical store. It makes sense: Your record of paying bills says a lot about how responsible you are with credit. Lenders want to know whether you pay on time and how long it's been since you've been late, if ever.

To put this in perspective: 6 out of 10 Americans don't have a single late payment on their credit reports, according to Fair Isaac.

When it comes to negative marks like late payments, the score focuses on three factors:

- **Recency**—This is how recently the borrower got into trouble. The more time that's passed since the credit problem, the less it impacts a score.

- **Frequency**—As you might expect, someone who has had just one or two late payments typically looks better to lenders than someone who has had a dozen.

- **Severity**—There's a definite "hierarchy of badness" when it comes to your credit score. A payment that's 30-days late isn't considered as serious as one that's 60- or 120-days late. Collections, tax liens, and bankruptcy are among the biggest black marks.

If you've never been late, your clean history will help your score. But that doesn't mean you'll get a "perfect" score. A good credit history involves a lot more.

How Much You Owe

This equates to 30 percent of your score. The score looks at the total amount owed on all accounts as well as how much you owe on different types of accounts (credit card, auto loan, mortgages, and so on).

To put this in perspective: The average American uses 32 percent of his or her available credit limits, according to Fair Isaac.

As you might expect, using a much higher percentage of your limits will worry lenders and potentially hurt your score. People who max out their credit limits, or even come close, tend to have a much higher rate of default than people who keep their credit use under control.

When it comes to revolving debt—credit cards and lines of credit—the credit score formula looks at the difference between your credit limits on the accounts and your balance, or the amount of credit you're actually using. The bigger the gap between your balance and your limit, the better.

Here's a point that needs clarification: Lenders report your balances to the credit bureaus on a given day (usually each month, but sometimes only every other month or quarterly). It doesn't matter if you pay the balance off in full the next day—the balance you owed on the reporting day is what shows up on your credit report. That's why people who pay off their credit cards in full every month still might have balances showing on their reports.

So you need to be careful with how much you charge, even if you never carry a balance from month to month. Your total balance during the month should never approach your credit limit if you want a good score.

The score also looks at how much you owe on installment loans (mortgages, auto loans) compared to what you originally borrowed. Paying down the balances over time tends to help your score.

How Long You've Had Credit

This is 15 percent of your total score. As such, it's generally much less important than the previous two factors, but it still matters. You can have a good score with a short history, but typically the longer you've had credit, the better.

To put this in perspective: The average American's oldest account has been established for about 14 years, according to Fair Isaac.

The score considers both of the following:

- The age of your oldest account

- The average age of all your accounts

Your Last Application for Credit

This is 10 percent of your overall score. Opening new accounts can ding your credit score, particularly if you apply for lots of credit in a short time and you don't have a long credit history.

To put this in perspective: The average American has not opened an account in 20 months.

The score factors in the following:

- How many accounts you've applied for recently

- How many new accounts you've opened

- How much time has passed since you applied for credit

- How much time has passed since you opened an account

You might have heard that "shopping around" for credit can hurt your score. We'll deal with this issue more thoroughly in the next chapter, but the FICO formula takes into account that people tend to shop around for important loans like mortgages and auto financing. As long as you do your shopping in a fairly concentrated period of time, it shouldn't affect the score used for your application.

Also, pulling your own credit report and score doesn't affect your score. As long as you do it yourself, ordering from a credit bureau or a reputable intermediary, the inquiry won't count against you. If you have a lender pull your score "just to see it," though, you could end up hurting your score.

The Types of Credit You Use

This is 10 percent of your score. The FICO scoring formula wants to see a "healthy mix" of credit, but Fair Isaac is customarily vague about that means.

The company does say that you don't need to have a loan of each possible type—credit card, mortgage, auto loan, and so on—to have a good score. Furthermore, you're cautioned against applying for credit you don't need in an effort to boost your score, because that can backfire.

To get the highest possible scores, though, you need to have both revolving debts like credit cards and installment debts like an auto loan, mortgage, or personal loan. These latter loans don't have to still be open to influence your score. But they do still need to show up on your credit report.

Bankcards—major credit cards such as Visa, MasterCard, American Express, Discover, and Diner's Club—are typically better for your credit score than department store or other "finance company" cards. (Department stores' cards are typically issued by finance companies, which specialize in consumer lending and which, unlike banks, don't receive deposits.)

Installment loans can reflect well on you, too. That's because lenders generally require more documentation and take a closer look at your credit before granting the loan.

To put this in perspective: The average American has four or five bankcards showing on their credit report, and most have at least one installment loan, according to Fair Isaac.

Your Credit Scorecard

How these five factors are weighed when it comes to *you*—as opposed to the general population—depends on a little-known sorting system known at Fair Isaac as "scorecards."

Scorecards allow the FICO formula to segment borrowers into one of 10 different groups, based on information in their credit reports.

If the credit history shows only positive information, the model takes into account the following:

• The number of accounts

• The age of the accounts

• The age of the youngest account

If the history shows a serious delinquency, the model looks for these:

- The presence of any public record, such as a bankruptcy or tax lien

- The worst delinquency, if there's more than one on the file

After the model has this information, it decides which of the 10 score-cards to assign. Although Fair Isaac keeps the details pretty secret, it's known that there is at least one scorecard for people with a bankruptcy in their back-grounds, and another for people who don't have much information in their reports.

Grouping people this way is supposed to enhance the formula's predictive power. The theory is that the same behavior in different borrowers can mean different things. Someone with a troubled credit history who suddenly opens a slew of accounts, for example, might be seen as a much greater risk that someone with a long, clean history. Scorecards allow the FICO formula to give different weight to the same information.

Sometimes, however, the actual results of the scorecards can be a little bizarre.

Naomi of Richmond, Virginia, spent years rebuilding her credit and couldn't wait for the seven-year mark to pass on three negative items on her credit report: two collection actions and a judgment. These items, she was sure, were the only things holding her credit score down.

When the black marks disappeared from her report, however, Naomi's score actually *dropped* more than 20 points.

Naomi got caught in what can be a jarring transition from one scorecard to the next.

The negative items on her credit report got her assigned to a certain scorecard, but her efforts to rebuild her credit—making payments on time and using credit responsibility—helped her rise to the top of that scorecard group.

When her negative marks disappeared, though, she was transferred to another group with tougher standards. In that group, she was closer to the bottom, and her credit score drop reflected her fall.

Fair Isaac says its NextGen formula eases this issue by segmenting bor-rowers into finer groups, which should lead to less dramatic tumbles from one group to the next.

In the meantime, Naomi's only solace is that the responsible credit behavior she's learned should help boost her score and recover lost ground over time.

Your Results Might Differ

There are a few more complications about which you need to know.

Although all three bureaus use the FICO scoring model, the actual formula differs slightly from bureau to bureau. That's because the way the bureaus collect and report data isn't exactly the same. It's unlikely that these differences would have much impact on your score, but you should know that they exist. You're far more likely, though, to have different scores from bureau to bureau because the underlying information is different.

As discussed earlier, lenders can have their own in-house scoring formulas in addition to, or instead of, using FICO scores. Lenders also can use different "editions" of the FICO formula. Just as not everyone updates to the latest computer operating systems when they're released, not every lender uses the latest versions of credit-scoring formulas.

Older versions of the FICO formula, for example, counted participation in a credit-counseling program as a negative factor; newer versions view it as a neutral factor. So, if you're currently in a debt management program, you might be viewed more negatively by some lenders than by others.

Just consider what happened to Marvin, a homebuyer who learned too late that his scores weren't what he thought they were.

Marvin purchased FICO scores from each of the three credit bureaus. Because lenders usually use the middle of your three scores to determine your interest rates, Marvin was happy to discover his middle score was 638—not great, but high enough to avoid the 620 mark many lenders use to classify a borrower as subprime, or high risk.

When Marvin applied for a loan, however, the lender told him his middle score was 593. It's not clear whether the lender was using an older FICO formula or was simply using its own modified concoction and calling it a FICO, but Marvin paid the price.

"No one tells you this when you pay your money to get your score,"
Marvin said. "We actually put our house on the market based on the
information we received from the agencies, having to scramble later for a
mortgage company to accept our lower score. We went from being able to
receive competitive interest rates to being considered very high risk and
receiving very high rates."

You can help protect yourself somewhat from these discrepancies by getting preapproved for a home loan before you start house shopping. But this is just another reason why it's important to improve and protect your score. The higher your score is, the less you have to worry about a few points making a difference.

How Do I Get My Score?

If you've surfed the Internet lately, you might find it hard to believe that credit scores were secret only a few short years ago. Sometimes it seems like every other Web site is either hawking credit scores or running an ad for a Web site that does.

As you've read, though, not all credit scores are created equal.

The credit bureaus, for example, sometimes market scores to consumers that aren't based on the FICO formula—the one typically used by lenders. The bureaus say these scores are a good indicator of a consumer's credit-worthiness, but their results can differ—sometimes markedly—from the FICO numbers that lenders use.

Your first step: Make sure you're getting a real FICO or NextGen score. If it doesn't say FICO or NextGen or use one of the credit bureau's trade-marked names for FICO scores (see below), it's not the same formula lenders use.

The FICO score has different names at the three major credit bureaus.

Credit Bureau	FICO Score Name
Equifax, Equifax Canada	Beacon
Experian	Experian/Fair Isaac Risk Model
TransUnion, TransUnion Canada	Empirica

Be careful not to be misled by pitches that promise "free" access to your credit score. Typically, those offers require signing up for credit monitoring or other ongoing services that are most assuredly not free. Although you might decide that these services are helpful, make sure to read the fine print so that you understand what you're getting and how you can cancel if necessary. Another caution: Some fly-by-night operators might pitch credit scores as a way to get you to reveal your private financial information, such as your Social Security number or credit card numbers. As always on the Web, it's best to do business with companies you know and to make sure you have a secure connection before transmitting sensitive information. Congress recently did give U.S. residents the right to get free copies of their credit reports annually from each of the three bureaus. But that doesn't include the right to free scores; the bureaus can and will continue to charge for those.

One place to look for your score is MyFICO.com, a joint venture between Fair Isaac and Equifax. The site offers your credit reports and FICO scores from each of the three bureaus for about $39. (One score and one report is $12.95.)

In Canada, you can get your FICO score from Equifax Canada.

If you don't have Internet access, your options for getting your FICO score are more limited. As of this writing, one company, called Intersections, Inc., offered FICO scores for U.S. residents that are based on TransUnion credit files. You can reach them at 800-695-7536.

Along with your score, MyFico.com provides a fever chart that shows where you stand in relation to other borrowers, along with a summary of how lenders are likely to view you as a credit risk.

In Figure 2.1, the borrower has an Experian FICO score of 776, which puts her ahead of about 75 percent of other Americans.

Figure 2.1 How you rank

Source: Fair Isaac Co. Used by permission.

MyFico.com goes on to tell you more what this means, saying in part:

Lenders consider many factors in addition to your credit score when making credit decisions. Looking solely at your FICO score, however, most lenders would consider this score as excellent.

This means: It is extremely unlikely your application for credit cards or for a mortgage or auto loan would be turned down, based on your score alone.

You should be able to obtain relatively high credit limits on your credit card.

Most lenders will consider offering you their most attractive and most competitive rates.

Many lenders will also offer you special incentives and rewards targeted to their "best" customers.

Source: MyFico.com

Figure 2.2 Your risk of default

Because the primary purpose of a FICO score is to predict default risk, you might be interested to know how you stack up in that regard. As you can see from the following chart, compiled by MyFico.com for a borrower with a FICO score of 700, the risk of fault rises dramatically as scores drop:

When you get your FICO, you should get a summary of the major positive and negative factors influencing your score. Be sure to read these carefully, along with any additional explanatory information. These factors are provided to give you some clues about how to improve your score, but if you misinterpret the results, you could end up making things worse.

For example, many people with good credit often find that one of the reasons their score isn't higher is that they have "too many credit cards." They think they can solve the problem by closing cards, but the FICO formula doesn't work that way. The closed cards remain on your credit report and continue to influence your score. In fact, the act of closing accounts can actually hurt your score, as I'll explain later, and can never help it.

The positive factors you'll see should be listed in order of importance, and might be something like the following:

- You have no late payments reported on your credit accounts.

- You demonstrate a relatively long credit history.

- You have a low proportion of balances to credit limits on your revolving/charge accounts.

Negative factors, too, should be listed in order of importance. If you have a bankruptcy, collections action, or other serious delinquency, that would be mentioned first. Other negatives that can show up for even the best borrowers include the following:

- You have recently been seeking credit or other services, as reflected by the number of inquiries posted on your credit file in the past 12 months.

- You have a relatively high number of consumer finance company accounts being reported.

- The proportion of balances to credit limits (high credit) on your revolving/charge accounts is too high.

- The length of time your accounts have been established is relatively short.

Now, nobody likes criticism, and some people get absolutely furious when they read through the reasons they're given for why their score isn't higher. Interestingly, many of these folks tend to have excellent credit, but—like Brian in the previous chapter—they're angry that their score isn't "perfect."

Understand that nobody is "perfect," and even if you could achieve a perfect score, the changing circumstances of your life and your credit use would mean you wouldn't keep that score for long.

Also understand that the negative reasons listed are less and less important the higher your score. The bureaus need to give you some reason for why your scores aren't higher, but when your score is already in the mid-700s and above, there's no guarantee that even if you could fix the "problem" that your scores would rise that much.

Still, you can always learn something from reading the reasons given. A notation that your balances are too high should spur you to pay down your debt, for your own financial health as well as for the sake of your score. Getting dinged for having too many cards should keep you from applying for yet another department store card just to get a 10 percent discount. You don't need one more piece of plastic to keep track of, anyway.

If your score is low, though, you should take the negative factors to heart. They can provide a blueprint for fixing your credit and boosting your score. In Chapter 3, "Improving Your Credit Score—The Right Way," you'll find general information about improving your score, and in later chapters, I'll discuss more specific strategies for people who have troubled credit.

3

IMPROVING YOUR SCORE— THE RIGHT WAY

Okay, now you know your score, and you have a good idea of what goes into creating it. So, how do you make it better?

Step 1: Start with Your Credit Report

Because your credit score is based on your credit report, you should begin by ordering your reports from all three credit bureaus and reviewing each one for accuracy. You can get your reports from a service such as MyFico.com, or order from each bureau separately online or by phone:

Equifax	*Experian*	*Trans Union*
www.equifax.com	www.experian.com	www.transunion.com
800-685-1111	888-397-3742	800-888-4213

Canadians can also get their credit reports online:

Equifax Canada	*Trans Union Canada*	*Northern Credit*
www.equifax.com	www.tuc.ca	*Bureaus, Inc.*
(click on the		www.creditbureau.ca
"Canada" link)		

If you're accessing your reports online, you might want to print out the files to make the review process easier. At the very least, grab some paper and a pen to make a list of the changes needed as you go through the reports.

Exactly how your information is organized varies from report to report. But the basic sections are pretty similar and proceed more or less in the order outlined in this chapter.

Check the Identifying Information

At the top of each report is identifying information about you. Watch especially for the following:

- Names that aren't yours (not just misspellings of your own name)

- Social Security numbers that don't belong to you

- An incorrect birth date

- Addresses where you have never lived

These are the kinds of errors that could indicate someone else's information is in your file.

You might find other errors, such as an employer listed that you no longer work for or a misspelled address. You can ask the bureau to fix those problems as well, but that shouldn't be your highest priority.

Carefully Review the Credit Accounts

The next section lists credit accounts that you've opened, along with such information as the date you opened them, whether the account is still open or now closed, the type of account, the account number (typically abbreviated), your payment history, your credit limits, and your balances.

Scan this section closely for the following:

- Accounts that aren't yours

- Delinquencies that aren't yours (including late payments and charge-offs)

- Late payments, charge-offs, or other negative entries—other than a bankruptcy—that are more than seven years old

- Debts that your spouse incurred before marriage (unless they improve your credit history—more on that later)

- Any other incorrect account notations, such as showing a debt as past due when it was wiped out in a bankruptcy filing

If you find a number of incorrect entries, especially if they're delinquent or unpaid accounts, you could be a victim of identity theft. You'll find more information about how to handle this situation in Chapter 7, "Identity Theft and You."

On the other hand, you could be suffering from a credit bureau mix-up that accidentally merged someone else's information with yours. Although the bureaus say they have improved their systems to reduce the chances of this happening, it still occurs. I hear about it most often when two family members share similar names.

Don B. and his father have the same first and last names and share a middle initial. They live in different states (Florida and Indiana, respectively) and, of course, have different Social Security numbers. That hasn't prevented the credit bureaus from getting the two men confused.

When Don bought a piece of property recently, the bank pulled his credit reports from all three bureaus. He discovered that his and his father's credit information had been mixed together.

"For example, his car payment is on my report, but my car payment does not show up on my own report," Don said. "I was shocked at the number of discrepancies I found on each of the reports. As important as one's credit history is, one would think that these agencies would take the necessary steps to ensure accuracy."

You might find other errors, such as accounts you've long since closed still being reported as open, or not indicating accurately that you—rather than the creditor—closed the account.

The FICO scoring system doesn't really care who closes accounts, so you needn't worry too much about fixing those notations. And don't rush to change the notation on your closed accounts if they're listed as active; as I'll explain later, they could be helping your credit score.

Parse Through Your Inquiries

Inquiries show who has asked to review your credit report. Your credit score doesn't count inquiries made by lenders looking to make preapproved credit offers or your own requests to see your credit history. These are known as *soft* inquiries.

The inquiries that matter are the ones from lenders that resulted from you applying for credit. These are called *hard* inquiries.

What you do want to look for are these:

- Credit inquiries older than two years

- Hard credit inquiries that you didn't authorize

Add these to your list of items to dispute with the credit bureaus.

Examine Your Collections and Public Records

The final section of your credit report includes any collection actions or public records—including bankruptcies, foreclosures, garnishments, lawsuit judgments, and tax liens. Here's what you want to look for here:

- Bankruptcies that are older than 10 years or that aren't listed by the specific bankruptcy code chapter (Chapter 7, Chapter 13, and so on).

- Lawsuits, judgments, or paid tax liens older than seven years.

- Paid liens or judgments that are listed as unpaid.

- Duplicate collections, such as a loan that's listed under more than one collection agency. (An account you didn't pay often is listed twice, once with the original creditor and once with a collection agency, but there shouldn't be more than one collector listed at a time for the same debt.)

- Any negative information that isn't yours.

If in this review process you didn't find errors of note, skip to the next step. If you did, read on.

Dispute the Errors

Your credit report comes with a form for disputing errors by mail (if you ordered by phone) or online, depending on the way you ordered your report.

Credit bureaus are required by law to investigate any mistakes you bring to their attention and report back to you within 30 days. Typically they ask the creditor that reported the information to check its records. If the creditor can't vouch for the accuracy of what it reported or doesn't respond, the offending item is deleted from your report.

That doesn't mean the error stays off. Unfortunately, some creditors persist in reporting inaccurate information. A consumer might follow the rules to get a problem removed, and the creditor simply reports it again a few months later.

That's what happened to Stan, a homeowner who encountered problems when his mortgage was transferred during a bank merger. The new bank made a mistake and reported to the credit bureaus that he was late with a $232 payment.

When Stan discovered the negative mark on his report, he contacted the bank and a representative agreed to fix the problem.

"She worked with me by giving me a letter stating [that the late payment was] reported in error," Stan said. Several months later, the late payment showed up again on his credit report. Stan contacted another bank official, who again promised to fix it after Stan faxed him the first representative's letter. When Stan pulled his report 60 days later, however, the delinquency was still there.

As you can see, the creditor holds a lot of power in this process. Although many errors are fixed promptly, permanently, and without fuss, an unethical or indifferent creditor could make your life difficult by *verifying* to the credit bureau that incorrect information is, in fact, accurate or simply rereporting an old error. If you run into this problem, check out the information in "What to Do If a Credit Bureau Won't Budge" in Chapter 7.

If you're successful in getting errors removed from your report, you might—or might not—notice an improvement in your credit score. It all depends on the information remaining. The following section presents the best and most effective ways to make sure that information reflects well on you—and in your score.

Step 2: Pay Your Bills on Time

If you're new to the idea of credit scoring, you might have no idea how damaging just one late payment can be. I got this email from Brenda, a woman in Douglasville, Georgia, who was flabbergasted that all of her recent efforts to improve her credit score could be undone by one unpaid bill:

> *"I recently had a score of 640. I was late on a payment for a personal loan, and now it's 555. I now know that I can't afford to be late again, but that shouldn't have dropped my score that much, should it?"*

Oh, yes. And the better your credit, the more a late payment can hurt.

Lenders are looking for any sign that you might default, and a late payment is often a good indicator that you're in financial trouble.

Because payment history makes up more than a third of the typical credit score, ensuring that your bills get paid on time—*all* the time—is essential.

Now, for those of you panicking over that credit card bill you sent in two days past the due date: You can stop sweating. Normally a payment has to be at least 30 days overdue for a creditor to report it to the bureaus.

That doesn't mean paying even a day late is a good idea, of course. Creditors increasingly are eager to slap their customers with late fees and jack up interest rates in response to late payments. Some have moved from due dates to due times; for example, a payment is considered late if it isn't in their hands by 1 p.m. on the date that it's due.

Furthermore, you can face higher interest rates on all your credit cards and your insurance policies if you fall behind with even one creditor. Many lenders and insurers periodically review their customers' credit reports and adjust their rates based on what they find.

You also can't skate on creditors that don't regularly report to credit bureaus. You might not have seen your cell phone account or your electric bill showing on your credit history, but that doesn't mean these vendors won't report your delinquencies if you don't pay them on time.

How to Make Sure Your Bills Get Paid on Time, All the Time

I occasionally get letters like the following, which try to put the blame for late payments on someone else:

> *"I recently checked my credit report after moving and found that my credit card company was reporting that I was 60 days over due. I'm*

absolutely certain I haven't received the bill for that card in several months, or I would have paid it. Aren't they required to give me some notice before they report information like that to the credit bureaus?"

This might be a shock to some folks, but the answer is no. *You're responsible for paying your bills whether you get a statement or not.* You need to keep track of what you owe to whom and make sure that everyone gets paid, even if the U.S. Postal Service falls down on the job.

Keeping track of these details also can help you detect identity theft. Some criminals like to steal credit card statements out of residential mailboxes. The bolder ones file a change-of-address form with the post office so that your mail gets redirected, allowing the bad guys to sort through it at their leisure.

To stay on top of what you owe and when, you should make a list of every bill you must pay each month and the date that it's due. (Although credit card due dates can vary, they're usually around the same time each month, give or take a few days.) Then list any bills that are due less regularly—every other month, every quarter, every six months, and annually.

Now, using either a paper calendar you can hang prominently on a wall or an electronic calendar in your computer, enter all your bills. Get in the habit of checking the calendar at least weekly to see what bills are coming up and to make sure they're all getting paid.

You can set up electronic reminders to help you as well:

- If you have a Palm or other personal data assistant, you can configure it to alert you.

- Many Internet Service Providers (ISPs), such as AOL and MSN, provide email reminder services.

- Bill-reminder features are part of personal finance software, such as Quicken and Money.

- Some credit cards, including Discover, email you when your bill is due.

If you really want to protect your credit, though, you should take further steps to avoid human error. The more of your bills that you put on automatic, the less worries you'll have about late payments, late charges, and dings on your bill.

There are a few options.

Automatic Payments

An automatic payment allows the companies that you owe to take their payments directly from your checking account each month, with no action on your part—no checkbook, no stamps, no fuss. This is my favorite way of paying bills, and it could be yours. Just muster up the guts to try it.

A lot of people balk at the idea of letting a mortgage lender, utility company, or other vendor have regular access to their bank accounts. Some feel it's somehow an invasion of privacy. In reality, the vendor can't "see" into your account or monitor what other activity is going on there. The money comes out basically the same way it would if you paid by check or by other electronic transfer.

A federal law prohibits vendors from taking out more than you authorize. If a mistake is made—and in more than a decade of paying bills automatically, it's only happened to me once—the company is obliged to replace the money it took in error.

Many people insist that they need control over when bills get paid. Typically, these folks have gotten into the bad habit of juggling bills or of not keeping enough cash in their checking account to cover their ongoing obligations. It's a good idea to always keep a "pad" of $500 to $1,000 in your checking account, regardless of how you pay your bills, and to sign up for overdraft protection on your checking account. These lines of credit, which usually cost less than $50 a year, can pay for themselves the first couple of times you avoid a bounced check.

Or perhaps you've fallen into another bad habit—not paying your credit card balances in full. If that's the case, be sure to read later about how that can hurt your credit score. In the meantime, know that most credit card companies have several automatic payment options. They can take out just the minimum payment or a set dollar amount each month instead of the full statement balance. If you opt for these partial payments, you can always pay more by check or online.

Really, you only have two choices: to pay your bills on time, or pay them late. If you want good credit and don't want to worry about missing due dates, automatic payments are the answer. You will still get a bill each month with plenty of time to correct any problems on the statement before the payment is made.

My suggestion to you is this: Try it. Pay one bill a month this way. You can start with a mortgage payment or a student loan, because these payments tend to be the same each month, and the lenders might even give you a break on the rate if you agree to automatic payments. Just phone your lender and ask whether they offer automatic payments. (Some call it "direct debit" or "direct payment.") If they do, they will send you a form to fill out. Do so, send it back, and you'll be on your way.

You'll probably soon find yourself converting more and more bills to automatic payment. Then you'll never again have to worry about forgetting a bill or missing a payment while you're on vacation.

Recurring Credit Card Charges

If you're not quite ready to let vendors have access to your checking account, you can have some of your bills charged automatically on your credit card.

Using a credit card can give you an extra layer of protection, because if a mistake is made, you have the credit card company to act as a middleman. You can dispute an erroneous charge and not have to pay it until the problem is resolved.

This method of paying bills comes with two rather large caveats, though:

- **You should try this only if you can pay off the card in full each month**—Paying credit card interest is rarely a good idea, but it's never advised when you're paying basic monthly expenses.

- **You should use this only with your smaller bills**—It matters to your credit score how much of your available credit you use, whether or not you pay your bill in full each month. If paying your bills would bring you anywhere close to your credit limit, you'll be hurting—not helping—your score.

Online Bill Payment

For those who really need that illusion of control or who pay vendors that don't offer other forms of automatic payment, online bill paying can be the answer.

You can set up your system so that you decide when each bill gets paid, but you also can set up recurring payments so that bills get paid automatically. The difference is that you, not the vendor, can decide when these recurring payments start and stop.

Of course, this works only for bills that are the same amount every month. Credit cards and other bills that vary require that you specify the amount that gets paid each month.

The downside of many online bill payment systems is the cost, which can range from $5 to $15 a month. Although many banks have wised up and now offer free online bill paying, others still insist on charging. If your bank does, you might nag them about making it free.

Online bill paying has another advantage, one shared by automatic charges. Electronic transactions leave excellent "trails" that can show exactly when the bill got paid, so there's never a question of a check getting lost in the mail. If you have a vendor that's constantly slapping you with late fees, and you suspect they're deliberately not processing your check, you can put a stop to those games with electronic payments.

What if none of the solutions thus far works for you? You have one more good option.

Just Pay Your Bills As They Come In

If you sit down and pay each bill immediately as it arrives, most of your worries about late payments will be solved. You'll still need a calendar to keep track of your statements and due dates to make sure a bill hasn't gone awry, but you won't have to worry about losing a notice in a pile of other paperwork.

Step 3: Pay Down Your Debt

Remember that the second most heavily weighted factor in credit scoring is how much of your available credit you're actually using. The lower your balances compared to your credit limits, the better.

The score gauges how much of your limit you use on each card or other revolving line of credit, as well as how much of your combined credit limits you're using on all your cards. The score also factors in any progress you're making on paying down installment accounts such as auto loans and mortgages.

Paying down your debt over time is a way to show consistent, responsible credit-handling behavior and will boost your score.

What does that mean in practice? Read on.

You Need to Reduce What You Owe, Rather Than Just Moving Your Balances Around

With credit card companies battling each other fiercely for customers and 0 percent balance transfer offers now commonplace, it has become quite a sport for some people to bounce their balances from one low-rate credit card to the next. These folks often are quite proud of the "savings" they think they're getting from taking advantage of such teaser rates.

Unfortunately, this strategy is fraught with peril. For one thing, opening new accounts can ding credit scores. So can transferring a balance from a high-limit card to a lower-limit card. (Remember: The more of your credit limit you use on any given card, the bigger the hit on your credit score.)

If you continue to charge on your cards instead of paying down your balances, you're using more and more of your available credit limit—and doing more and more damage to your score.

The way to improve your score is to stop the merry-go-round and start actually making a dent in your debt. To do that, continue reading.

You Might Need to Change Your Approach to Paying Off Debt

The usual advice to debt-ridden consumers is that they should pay off their highest-rate debts first, and use lump sums to retire any bills they can afford to pay off in full. That makes a lot of financial sense, but unfortunately isn't the fastest way to improve your credit score. Instead, you should do this:

- **Prioritize your debts by how close the balances are to the accounts' credit limits**—If boosting your score is your goal, you should look for the card or other revolving account that's closest to its limit. After that's paid down below 30 percent or so, you can switch to the card or other account that's the second closest to its limit. Your goal should be to eventually pay off all this debt, continuing in this round-robin fashion.

- **Avoid consolidating your debts**—Many people want to transfer their balances to a single card, either to take advantage of a low rate or for the convenience of having only one due date and interest rate to worry about. But for credit scoring purposes, it's better to have small balances on a number of cards than a large balance on one card or other revolving line of credit. That's because the score looks at the gap between the balance and the limit on each card, as well as on all your cards put together.

If you've already consolidated, though, you should probably just stay put. Applying for new credit or transferring balances, as noted earlier, can hurt your score and offset any gain you might get.

If you think all this doesn't apply to you because you never carry a balance, think again.

You Need to Pay Attention to How Much You Charge—Even If You Pay Your Balances Off in Full Every Month

As noted in the previous chapter, the credit bureaus—and thus your credit scores—don't differentiate between the balances you pay off and those you carry from month to month. The balances that are reported to the bureaus are typically the ones that show up on the monthly statements you're sent. Even if you pay off your bill in full the day your statement arrives, you will likely still have balances showing on your credit report, and those will be factored into your score.

Now, paying your balances in full every month is an excellent financial habit. If you're not doing it already, that should be your goal. Not carrying a balance can save you hundreds, if not thousands, of dollars a year in interest payments. Besides, carrying a balance leaves you vulnerable to all kinds of nasty creditor tricks, like jacking up your interest rates with little warning— something that's increasingly common as credit card issuers try to boost their profits.

But even if you can and do pay your balances off, you need to pay attention to how much you're charging each month. You need to stay below—well below—your credit limits.

You know by now that you shouldn't max out your cards or come anywhere close to your credit limits. But the amount of your credit limit you should be using might surprise you.

Your balances (the amount you carry plus the amount you charge) shouldn't exceed 30 percent of your total credit limit at any given time. The higher your score, the lower the percentage of your credit limits you would need to use to improve your numbers. If your score is already in the high 700s or 800s, you might need to use 10 percent or less of your limit to boost your score.

How to Find Money to Pay Down Your Debt

Paying down debt is a lot like losing weight—easier said than done. But most people can find ways to trim their expenses, boost their incomes, and free up more money to pay off their debts. Here are just a few examples. You can find lots more on Web sites devoted to frugality, such as The Dollar Stretcher at www.stretcher.com, or in books such as Amy Dacyczyn's *The Tightwad Gazette*.

- **You can sell stuff**—Hold a yard sale, take clothes to consignment shops, sell unneeded vehicles, and auction off unneeded items on eBay. The money generated might go a long way toward paying off your debts.

- **You can trim your spending**—The easiest ways to save are to eat out less often, shop using a grocery list, and entertain yourself at home rather than going out, but you probably can find several other places in your budget to trim. Personal finance software, such as Quicken or Money, can help you track your spending, but you also can try just writing down every penny you spend for a couple of weeks. You're bound to find little ways that money leaks out of your wallet. Stop those holes, and you can redirect the savings toward debt.

- **You can moonlight**—Few people would want to hold two jobs for long, but you might be able to handle it for several months or however long it takes to put a dent in your debt.

Step 4: Don't Close Credit Cards or Other Revolving Accounts

If your goal is to improve your credit score, don't close any of your current accounts. Closing credit cards and other revolving accounts can *never* help your score, and it might actually hurt it.

Shutting down accounts reduces your total available credit, and that makes your balances loom larger. That narrowing of the gap between the credit you're using and the total credit available to you is one of the things that can hurt your score.

Closing older accounts can also hurt you, because the formula notes both the age of your oldest account and the average age of all your accounts. It's particularly important to keep your oldest account active, because shutting it could make your credit history look years younger than it actually is—and your score could drop as a result.

It may not be enough, by the way, to keep your oldest credit card in a drawer. If you don't charge something occasionally, your lender could decide the inactive account is more trouble than it's worth and close it for you. To keep it active, you might want to charge some small, recurring bill to the card—a newspaper subscription, your health club dues—and arrange to have the balance paid off automatically each month.

Step 5: Apply for Credit Sparingly

Responsible credit users don't apply for credit they don't need. They also try to pace their credit requests, so that they're not opening a bunch of accounts in a short period of time.

Although your first few credit accounts serve to build and improve your credit history, there comes a point when each subsequent credit application can reduce your score. Where that point is, no one knows for sure; all Fair Isaac will say is that it depends on the other information in your file.

That shouldn't keep you from applying for a car loan if you need a new vehicle, or getting or refinancing a mortgage. But if you already have three or four major bankcards, you should think twice before applying for another one.

You also should resist the urge to apply for those "instant" accounts retail stores are always pushing. Sure, you might save 10 percent on your current purchase, but you could wind up paying more in overall interest if the application lowers your score.

How to Get a Credit Score If You Don't Have Credit

You might have heard that you need credit to get credit. It can certainly feel that way if you've ever applied for credit and been turned down for lack of a credit history.

But people establish credit all the time, and you can do so fairly quickly if you follow the following steps.

If you're a parent with a teen, you might want to help your child through this process as a way to teach them responsible credit use. As noted later, your student will be able to get credit easily when he or she is in college; more than 80 percent of college students have at least one card. The best time for students to learn about credit is while they're at home, under your supervision—and long before they pass by their first credit card sign-up booth on campus.

Check Your Credit Report, If You Have One

You might think you have no record at the credit bureaus, but you could be wrong.

Charles, an 18-year-old in Moline, Illinois, was turned down when he applied for his first credit card. He pulled his report and was shocked to find a collection action. It turns out that his parents had placed a newspaper ad for him while he was still a minor and then forgot to pay the bill.

The collection never should have appeared on his report. Minors can't be held to contracts and therefore are typically not responsible for debts. But the time to detect and fix the problem was before Charles applied for credit.

Another problem you might run into is identity theft. Part of the surge of recent ID fraud cases involves thieves who use children's Social Security numbers to get credit, said Robert Ellis Smith, editor of *Privacy Journal*. This kind of theft can go on for years before being detected.

If that's happened to you, you need to clean up your credit report before trying to apply for new accounts. See Chapter 7 for help.

Set Up Checking and Savings Accounts

These usually don't show up on your credit report, but lenders see them as important signs of financial responsibility and stability. They are also one of the few steps you can take as a minor to start building a financial history, because you won't be able to apply for credit in your own name until you're 18.

Getting a debit card can give you some practice in using plastic. Debit cards are ATM cards with a Visa or MasterCard logo. You can use them with a personal identification number or PIN, or you can use them like a credit card just by signing a charge slip. The amounts you charge are deducted directly from your checking account.

Nan Mead, communications director for the National Endowment for Financial Education, got her son a debit card in the sixth grade. She put a month's worth of money into the account at a time and made him responsible for managing his allowance, lunch money, and incidental expenses, such as haircuts and school supplies.

"As I knew he would, he went through the first month's money during his first week of school. He bought CDs, pizza for all of his friends," Mead said. "I declined to bail him out, so he ended up taking a sack lunch to school for the rest of the month—a very uncool thing to do at that age, of course—and he had no discretionary money left to spend, either. His money management skills improved each month, though, until, by Christmas, he was doing quite well, even saving for some short-term goals."

As a college freshman, Mead's son received a credit card with a $500 limit. So far, so good, she says.

"In retrospect, the debit card was probably one of the best things I've done, in terms of providing a financial lesson to my son," Mead said. "The mistakes he made initially were small, in the overall scheme of things, and he learned from them. When he graduates to one or more unrestricted credit cards, I believe he will do just fine."

Use Someone Else's Good Name

You might be able to jumpstart your credit history by being added to someone else's credit card as an authorized or joint user. Typically, the history for that account will be imported onto your credit report. That can be a wonderful boost if the person who's adding you is responsible with credit.

If not, though, the results can be disastrous.

Angie P., a Kansas college student, learned that the hard way. Her mother added her as a joint user on a credit card and then failed to pay the bill for more than two months when money grew tight over the holidays. Angie only discovered the delinquency when she checked her credit report.

"I'm just worried an employer will look at my [credit score, now 637] and think I'm irresponsible because of this mess!" Angie said. "What's worse—I'm an accounting and finance major, and this makes it look like I don't know how to handle my money."

If you're added as an authorized user, you're not responsible for paying the bill. But the original user's mistakes could still show up in your credit file. So if your goal is to establish good credit quickly, pick someone who has been responsible with credit and is likely to continue that behavior in the future.

Another strategy to start a credit history is to get someone with good credit to cosign a loan with you. The cosigner is taking a considerable risk, because if you fail to pay, the delinquencies show up on the other person's credit report. But sometimes soft-hearted relatives or friends are willing to take this chance.

Apply for Credit While You're a College Student

It will never be easier for you to get an unsecured credit card than while you're in school. Lenders are much more lenient about extending credit during the college years, because they know your parents are likely to pay your bills if you can't—and that parental support typically ends with graduation.

One reader told me that she lectured her daughter against the evils of credit cards and advised her to steer clear while she was in college. After the younger woman got out of school, though, the very lenders who had been falling all over themselves to offer her cards were now turning down her applications.

So get a card while you're in school, but choose it carefully. Look for the lowest available annual fee and interest rate. And don't go overboard—one or two major bankcards (Visa, MasterCard, American Express, or Discover) should be enough for now.

Apply for an Alternate Card

If you can't get a regular credit card, consider applying for a gas or department store charge card, which are typically fairly easy to get.

You also might consider a secured credit card. These cards require that you make a deposit with a bank (usually $200 to $1,000), and your credit limit is typically limited to that deposit amount. The best cards don't charge application fees, have low annual fees, and convert to a regular, unsecured card after a year or so. Web sites, such as Bankrate.com, offer lists of secured cards, including their rates and terms.

Make sure in advance that the lender reports to the credit bureaus. You can't build a credit history if the lender isn't reporting your payments.

Get an Installment Loan

After you've used plastic responsibly for several months, you might try for a small auto or personal loan. Because the credit scoring formula wants to see that you can responsibly handle different types of credit, adding an installment loan to your mix of credit cards can boost your score.

Amanda got her first credit card at 18, two weeks after she moved out of her parents' house. The card had a $200 limit and an atrocious 19.8 percent interest rate, but Amanda used it strictly to build her credit history by buying groceries and paying the bill off in full each month.

After six months, she got a credit card with a more reasonable interest rate and a higher limit. Three months after that, she got a used car loan for $6,000.

> *"Not bad for an 18-year-old," she said. "A year later, I got a gold credit card with a 12.9 percent [interest rate]."*

Today, Amanda checks her credit reports and scores every three months. She enjoys watching her credit score rise, and it motivates her to continue her good financial habits. She just wished more of her peers knew what she knows.

"If parents would address the credit issues with their children," Amanda said, *"and explain the importance of establishing a good credit history and of using credit wisely and responsibly, then maybe there wouldn't be so many problems."*

Credit Scores Without Credit

Lenders know there's a big market of the "credit underserved"—people with nonexistent or thin credit histories. Fair Isaac estimates that more than 50 million Americans either have no credit bureau files or have too little information in their files to generate a classic or NextGen FICO credit score.

Some mortgage lenders have been experimenting with ways to tap that market by using new approaches to gauging creditworthiness, such as monitoring whether an applicant has paid rent or utilities on time.

It was only a matter of time before Fair Isaac figured out a way to capitalize on the situation. In mid-2004, Fair Isaac introduced the FICO Expansion Score, which uses nontraditional information sources to create credit scores for people who don't already have credit. These sources include

- Payday lenders

- Check monitoring companies (the ones banks notify if you bounce too many checks)

- Retail purchase payment plans (such as rent-to-own programs)

Fair Isaac says it has enough of this nontraditional data to provide scores of half of the underserved population, or 25 million people.

It remains to be seen how quickly lenders will adopt the new score—and how accurate the underlying information will be. But this expansion of credit and credit scoring just underlines how important it is to adopt responsible money habits, such as paying your bills on time and managing your bank accounts so you don't bounce checks.

4

Credit Scoring Myths

For most of credit scoring's history, the vast majority of the people involved in lending decisions pretty much had to guess what hurt or helped a score. Creators of scoring formulas didn't want to reveal much about how the models worked, for fear that competitors would steal their ideas or that consumers would figure out how to beat the system.

Fortunately, today we know a lot more about credit scoring—but not everybody has kept up with the latest intelligence. Mortgage brokers, loan officers, credit bureau representatives, credit counselors, and the media, among others, continue to spread outdated and downright false information. Acting on their bad advice can put your score and your finances at significant risk.

Here are some of the most common myths.

Myth 1: Closing Credit Accounts Will Help Your Score

This one sounds logical, especially when a mortgage broker tells you that lenders are suspicious of people who have lots of unused credit available to them. What's to keep you, after all, from rushing out and charging up a storm?

Of course, if you think about it, what's kept you from racking up big balances before now? If you've been pretty responsible with credit in the past, you're likely to continue to be pretty responsible in the future. That's the basic principle behind credit scoring: It rewards behaviors that show moderate, responsible use of credit over time, because those habits are likely to continue.

The score also punishes behavior that's not so responsible, such as applying for a bunch of credit you don't need. Many people with high credit scores find that one of the few marks against them is the number of credit accounts listed on their reports. When they go to get their credit scores, they're told that one of the reasons their score isn't even higher is that they have "too many open accounts." Many erroneously assume they can "fix" this problem by closing accounts.

But after you've opened the accounts, you've done the damage. You can't undo it by closing the account.

You can, however, make matters worse. Closing accounts can hurt you in two ways:

- Closing accounts can make your credit history look younger than it is. Your credit score factors in the age of your oldest account and the average age of all your accounts. So closing accounts, particularly older accounts, can ding your score.

- Closing accounts reduces the total credit available to you, making your debt utilization ratio soar. Remember that the FICO formula measures the gap between the credit you use and your total credit limits. The wider the gap, the better. If you suddenly lower that limit by shutting down accounts, the gap narrows—and that's a bad thing.

This is true whether or not you keep a balance on your credit cards or pay them off in full every month. Remember: The FICO formula doesn't differentiate between balances that are carried and those that are paid off.

In reality, closing revolving credit accounts can *never* help your score, and it might hurt it.

Every time I write this fact, I get flooded with letters from mortgage brokers insisting I'm wrong. But every time Fair Isaac has investigated a case where a lending professional claimed a closure helped a score, it discovered that some other factor was actually responsible.

Sometimes the change was fairly obvious, such as a negative mark that passed the seven-year limitation and was dropped from the report. More often, the difference in scores was the result of something subtler, such as lower balances being reported on the borrower's accounts or the simple passage of time. (Remember: The longer it's been since you opened your first account and your last account, and the longer you've been paying on time, the better the effect on your score.)

This doesn't mean that you should never close a credit card or other revolving account. You might want to get rid of a card that's charging you an annual fee or shut down a few unused accounts to reduce the chances they could be hijacked by an identity thief. If your score is already in the mid-700s or higher, you should be fine closing a few accounts—as long as they're not your oldest cards. Otherwise, though, you'd be smart just to leave those accounts open until your score improves.

There are other good reasons to close accounts. If you have a serious spending problem, you might find cutting up and canceling your credit cards is the only way to keep yourself in line. If that's true, your credit score is probably the least of your worries.

You also might encounter one of those lenders who is spooked by open credit card accounts and demands that you close some. If the loan is big enough, like a mortgage, and the lender has already committed to giving you the money, you might have to take the risk to get your loan. But don't close accounts as a pre-emptive measure and endanger your score.

Myth 2: You Can Boost Your Score By Asking Your Credit Card Company to Lower Your Limits

This one is a variation on the idea that reducing your available credit somehow helps your score by making you seem less risky to lenders. Once again, it's off the mark.

Narrowing the gap between the credit you use and the credit you have available to you can have a negative effect on your score. It doesn't matter that you asked for the reduction; the FICO formula doesn't distinguish between lower limits that you requested and lower limits imposed by a creditor. All it sees is less space between your balances and your limits, and that's not good.

If you want to help your score, tackle the problem from the other end: by paying down your debt. Increasing the gap between your balance and your credit limit has a positive effect on your score.

Myth 3: You Can Hurt Your Score By Checking Your Own Credit Report

Hans, a doctor, emailed me in a panic after talking with his lender.

"I heard from our mortgage officer at our state employees' credit union that if you access your credit report too often—even just to clean it up— that it looks unfavorable to lenders. How can I then run a check safely to clean it up in preparation for our 'dream home' mortgage?"

Shortly after receiving that email, I received this perky little admonition from Lisa in East Wenatchee, Washington—yet another misinformed "expert":

"As a real estate agent with 20+ years of sales experience, I appreciate the information you shared [on CNBC today] with the home-buying consumer. However, your advice for the consumer to check their 'credit report often…' needs to be modified. Each and every time consumers check their credit reports, it actually lowers their credit scores! I have had clients check their credit on a weekly basis, only to have their FICO scores lowered by as much as 50 points!!!"

No amount of exclamation points makes it so, Lisa. Next to the myth about closing accounts, the myth that you can hurt your score just by checking your credit report seems to be the most pervasive—and potentially destructive.

You need to check your credit report and your score fairly frequently to make sure all is right with your financial world. Checking once a year is about the minimum; given the prevalence of identity theft, you might want to check in with all three bureaus at least twice a year. You should definitely pull all three reports and scores a few months before applying for new credit, because it can take awhile to correct any errors you find.

The folks at Fair Isaac understand your need to review your own data, which is why the FICO formula ignores any inquiries generated when you check your own reports and scores.

Where you can hurt yourself is if you ask a lender to check your score. When a lender pulls your credit, it generates what's known as "hard" inquiry—and those are counted against your score.

As long as you order from a credit bureau or a service affiliated with a bureau, such as MyFico.com, your inquiries won't hurt your score.

Myth 4: You Can Hurt Your Score By Shopping Around for the Best Rates

The folks propagating this particular myth might have an ulterior motive. After all, if you don't know what the competition is offering, how will you know if you got a good deal?

Creators of scoring formulas know that smart consumers want to shop around for the best rates, particularly on cars and homes. That's why the FICO formula lumps all mortgage- and auto-related inquiries made within 14 days and counts it as one inquiry. Furthermore, any inquiries made in the 30 days before the score is created are ignored. If you do your shopping for a car loan or mortgage in a concentrated period of time and get the loan before the 30-day window is up, you should be fine. Even if it takes a little longer than 30 days to get your loan approved, as often happens with mortgages, you should be okay if your rate-shopping was confined to a two-week period.

What you don't want to do is drag the process out over several weeks or open credit cards right before you plan to get a mortgage or a car loan. The "deduplification" process—that's what Fair Isaac calls it—only gives special treatment to inquiries that are car- or mortgage-related.

You can protect yourself further and make the shopping process easier by doing some research before you contact any lenders. Get your reports and scores so that you know where you stand, and then check Internet sites, such as MyFico.com or Bankrate.com, to see the kind of rates you can expect to get, given your score. That way you'll be able to tell a good deal from a bad one when it's offered.

By the way, speaking of bad deals, you should be careful not to give any credit or other personal financial information to a car dealership until you're ready to buy the car. Readers have reported finding dozens of inquiries on their credit reports after having casually visited a dealership or two. Although multiple inquiries made on the same day might not affect your score that much because they're all lumped together by the FICO formula, a page of inquiries might unnerve any lender who actually looks at your report.

People who have poor credit need to be particularly vigilant about inquiries. Although someone who has a good score might lose less than 5 points from a single inquiry (or a group of inquiries within 14 days), the impact can be greater for someone who has a troubled, sparse, or brief credit history. Repeatedly trying for loans and being turned down can take a toll on your score over time. Just read what happened to Chris in Asheville, North Carolina:

"Over the years, as I have struggled with my credit, I have tried several times to buy a car. Each time I have applied for credit, the car lot has run my credit at about 15 different [lenders] trying to get me a loan. Multiply this over the last two years (I know that's how long inquiries stay on your report) times two cars per year, and I have about a page and a half of inquiries. Now, this has had a dramatic effect on my credit score."

Actually, it's highly unlikely that inquiries alone are devastating Chris' score. It's more likely that his past credit troubles are still having an effect. But Chris certainly isn't making things better. Rather than give his score a chance to recover and improve, he keeps trying every six months, inflicting fresh injury.

Because his score is already poor, each new inquiry or group of inquiries is likely to hurt more than it might had he enjoyed a better score.

A better course for Chris and others who have poor scores is to give up on the idea of a car loan for a while and concentrate on improving their FICOs. Paying their bills on time, paying down any debt they have and getting and using a secured credit card should help their scores. After their numbers are out of the cellar, they can shop for loans without drastically impacting their scores.

Myth 5: You Don't Have to Use Credit to Get a Good Credit Score

Some people are so suspicious of credit that they advise giving up credit cards and living on a cash-only basis. They acknowledge that most people need mortgages and auto loans, but they feel the best way to impress a lender is by living a credit-free life.

Now that you know something about how credit scoring works, you can see the holes in this theory. The credit scoring formula is designed to judge how well you handle credit over time; if you have no credit, or you don't at least occasionally use the credit you have, the formula won't have enough information to make an assessment. You don't have to live in *debt* to get a decent score, but you do need to use credit.

In the past, some people were able to get high credit scores without having much credit. Earlier incarnations of the FICO credit score gave scores over 700 to some people with just one or two recently opened accounts. The newer versions of the formula, however, make it much tougher to get a lofty score if you have a thin credit history.

You probably need to be concerned about your score even if you have no plans to take out loans. Now that insurers are using credit information for underwriting and rating decisions, your failure to maintain a credit history could cost you in the form of higher premiums.

It's too bad that conscientious people who simply don't like debt should be punished with higher premiums, and some states have even banned insurers from using a lack of credit history as a reason to raise rates. If your state hasn't prohibited the practice, though, you might want to dust off your credit card and use it once in awhile.

Myth 6: You Have to Pay Interest to Have a Good Credit Score

This is the exact opposite of the previous myth, and it's just as misguided.

You don't need to carry a balance on your credit cards and pay interest to have a good score. As you've read several times already, your credit reports—and thus the FICO formula—make no distinction between balances you carry month to month and balances that you pay off. Smart consumers don't carry credit card balances for any reason, and certainly not to improve their scores.

Now, it is true that to get the highest FICO scores, you need to have both *revolving accounts*, such as credit cards, and *installment loans*, such as a mortgage or car loan. And with the exception of those 0 percent rates used to push auto sales after Sept. 11, most installment loans require paying interest.

But here's a news flash: You don't need to have the *very highest score* to get good credit. Any score over 720 or so is going to get you the best rates and terms with the vast majority of lenders. You'll have all the credit you need, and then some.

If you're trying to improve a mediocre score, a small, affordable install-ment loan can help—provided that you can get approved for it and pay it off on time. But otherwise there's no reason to get yourself into debt and pay interest.

Myth 7: Adding a 100-Word Statement to Your File Can Help Your Score If You Have an Unresolved Dispute with a Lender

Dave in Los Angeles wound up in a protracted fight with his phone compa-ny, which for months billed him for a phone line that, in fact, never worked. He went round and round with the company's technical service, customer service, and billing department. Finally, he gave up, refusing to pay the bill—even when it went into collections and onto his credit report. Dave figured he could offset the damage to his credit by sending the credit bureaus a 100-word statement explaining the problem.

Federal law does give you the right to have such statements attached to your credit file. Unfortunately, the credit scoring formula can't read—at least not in the traditional sense. It calculates scores based on how items on your credit report are coded, and these 100-word statements aren't coded at all, so they're not counted.

It's not clear how helpful such statements were before credit scoring became so widespread, but they're certainly not much help now.

Given how damaging late payments, collections, and other recent nega-tive marks are on your score, you want to avoid them if at all possible. This doesn't necessarily mean you have to give in and pay a bill that's clearly in error. But you also shouldn't let a $30 spat with your book club escalate into a collection that could trash your score. You might have to pay the bill under protest and then sue the vendor in small claims court.

Fortunately, most credit disputes can be solved well short of that. If you used a credit card to purchase something that didn't work, you can use the credit card company's dispute resolution process as outlined on the back of your statements. Patient, polite persistence with a company's customer service department can also help, as can a willingness to seek out supervisors or regulators who might be able to cut through a log jam.

If the collection has already landed on your report, follow the steps in Chapter 6, "Rebuilding Your Score After a Credit Disaster," to minimize or eliminate the impact.

Myth 8: Your Closed Accounts Should Read "Closed By Consumer," Or They Will Hurt Your Score

The theory behind this myth is that lenders will see a closed account on your credit report and, if not informed otherwise, will assume that a disgusted creditor cut you off because you screwed up somehow.

Of course, as you know by now, many lenders never see your actual report. They're just looking at your credit score, which couldn't care less who closed a credit card. Fair Isaac figures that if a lender shuts down your account, it's either for inactivity or because you defaulted. If you defaulted, that will be amply documented in the account's history.

If it makes you feel better to contact the bureaus and ensure that accounts you closed are listed as "closed by consumer," by all means do so. But it won't make any difference to your credit score.

Myth 9: Credit Counseling Is Worse Than Bankruptcy

Sometimes this is phrased as "credit counseling is as bad as bankruptcy" or "credit counseling is as bad as Chapter 13 bankruptcy." None of these statements is true.

A bankruptcy filing is the single worst thing you can do to your credit score. By contrast, the current FICO formula completely ignores any reference to credit counseling that might be on your credit report. Credit counseling is treated as a neutral factor, neither helping nor harming your score.

Credit counselors, in case you're not familiar with the term, specialize in negotiating lower interest rates and working out payment plans for debtors that might otherwise file for bankruptcy. Although credit counselors might consolidate the consumer's bills into one monthly payment, they don't offer loans—as debt consolidators do—or promise to eliminate or settle debts for less than the principal amount you owe.

The fact that credit counseling itself won't affect your score does not mean, however, that enrolling in a credit counselor's debt management plan will leave your credit unscathed.

Some lenders will report you as late just for enrolling in a debt management plan. Their reasoning is that you're not paying them what you originally owed, so you should have to suffer some pain.

That's not the only way you could be reported late. As you'll read in the next chapter, not all credit counselors are created equal, and some have been accused of withholding consumer payments that were intended for creditors. The missing payments showed up as "lates" on the consumers' credit reports, hurting their scores.

Finally, some lenders—particularly mortgage lenders—do indeed view current participation in a credit counseling program as the equivalent of a Chapter 13 bankruptcy. If they see it mentioned on a credit report, they won't extend credit as long as the notation of credit counseling remains on the borrower's file. But typically such notations are dropped as soon as the borrower completes the repayment plan. By contrast, a Chapter 13 bankruptcy can be reported for 7 years or more. (A Chapter 7 bankruptcy, which involves erasing your debts rather than retiring them with a repayment plan, stays on your report for up to 10 years.)

Credit counseling isn't something you should sign up for just because you want a lower interest rate or one place to send your payments instead of many. But, if you're behind on your debts or able to pay only the minimums, and you want an alternative to bankruptcy, you shouldn't stay away because of myths about its long-term impact on your credit.

Myth 10: Bankruptcy Hurts Your Score So Much That It's Impossible to Get Credit

Bankruptcy does deal a devastating blow to your score, but that doesn't mean you can't get credit afterward—or even that you'll have to wait that long.

You can get a mortgage in as little as six months after your bankruptcy is discharged (completed). You might get credit card offers before your case has even closed.

How quickly you'll re-establish credit and how much you'll pay for it will depend largely on your behavior after you file for bankruptcy. If you start handling credit responsibly—paying your bills on time, not running up big balances, and not applying for a bunch of credit at once—your score will begin to recover.

But it also will matter which lenders you approach for credit. Most mainstream lenders shun people who have filed for bankruptcy—sometimes just for the first few years, although sometimes for as long as the bankruptcy remains on your file.

Other lenders specialize in what's known as "subprime" borrowers—those with less-than-perfect credit, including bankrupts. You'll have to be careful, because some subprime lenders charge outrageous rates and fees. But you most likely will be able to get the loans you need if you search.

John, a military man stationed in Texas, said he and his wife were able to buy a house one year after their Chapter 7 bankruptcy filing and have been approved for other accounts, including a credit card and a cell phone. Buying a car has proved more of a challenge.

> *"It doesn't seem like my credit score is increasing at all. I say that because I applied to buy a Jeep last week and got turned down. A couple of months ago, I tried to buy a motorcycle and was turned down. What else can I do to increase my score?"*

Actually, the couple's credit scores probably are increasing—they just haven't gotten high enough for a mainstream auto lender to take a chance. Chris of Knoxville tried a different approach after filing for bankruptcy along with his wife:

> *"About two months after our discharge, we tried to buy a used car. We tried about five different banks and were turned down by each one,"* Chris wrote. *"A couple of months later, Saturn was having a 'second chance' type of sale [for people with troubled credit]. We were able to purchase at a higher interest rate. We were a little disappointed [at the rate] but grateful that we were able to purchase a nice family car to rebuild our credit."*

Corey of Hermitage, Tennessee, filed for bankruptcy in 2001. Within two years, Corey had graduated from secured credit cards (which require a deposit) to regular credit cards and auto loans.

> *"Sure, it has been very hard to get credit sometimes. The only credit card I could get [at first] was one from Providian Financial, and even then it had to be a secured one; however, the pain has been worth it. I have since turned that secured credit card into an unsecured one. Providian issued me another [card], and then Merrick Bank issued me one. I have also been able to acquire two car loans, my most recent one for my 2001 Nissan Xterra for $23,000 and at a 10 percent interest rate.*
>
> *The rates on my car loan and credit card could be better; however, I have no financial debt now other than my car and student loans, and I even have a great paying job with some money in the bank now."*

For more information on how best to rebuild after bankruptcy or other credit disaster, see Chapter 5, "Coping with a Credit Crisis."

5

Coping with a Credit Crisis

A credit crisis—being unable to manage your debts—can come on slowly as the result of overspending for many years. The balances on your accounts grow and grow; pretty soon you're able to make only the minimum payments, and then not even that.

Other times a credit crisis comes at you in a rush as a result of another financial setback—a job loss, a divorce, a major illness. Suddenly, you have more "outgo" than "income," and you're not sure where to turn.

A friend I'll call Charlie experienced a crisis that resulted from a combination of both forces. For years, he'd made a successful living as an animator, earning as much as a quarter million dollars a year. He and his family didn't have to worry much about money, because so much was flowing their way.

Like hundreds of others in his field, though, he was caught in the industry's downturn at the beginning of the millennium. By the time he contacted me, he had been unemployed for more than a year.

His primary concern was how he could get his home refinanced so that he could lower his interest rate and reduce his monthly expenses. Among the problems, though, was that he and his wife had pretty mediocre credit scores and, of course, very little income—just what he could scrape together from occasional freelance gigs.

Upon further discussion, there turned out to be an even bigger issue. The couple had taken out a $150,000 line of credit on their Los Angeles home— and spent every dime on living expenses. Not only had the line of credit run dry, but the payments were starting to be a strain, and the maxed-out account was really dampening their credit scores.

Charlie's situation was unusual only in the amount of debt he'd managed to rack up. I hear from hundreds of other people every month who are similarly struggling with serious credit and financial problems.

Many are hoping for some quick, magical fix. Some ask if they should get a debt consolidation loan, use credit counseling, or tap their retirement funds. Jeff of Fair Lawn, New Jersey, is fairly typical. At 44, he's accumulated more than $40,000 in credit card debt and is finding it tough to pay much more than the minimum balances he owes:

"I am seriously considering a disbursement [from a prior employer's 401(k)] to pay off my credit card bills. I understand there would be 20 percent withheld immediately, and a 10 percent early withdraw penalty next year at tax time. I'm still young enough to put future earnings aside for my retirement. I'm ready to make the leap. Am I wrong with this assessment? So much cash goes from my income straight to the credit card banks that it seems to be a viable alternative. What do you think?"

Kathy of Chapel Hill, North Carolina has $20,000 in credit card debt, racked up during a tumultuous period when her husband became disabled, a parent died, and she lost her job. She has enough equity in her home to pay the debt, but she can't find a lender willing to lend her the money to refinance.

"I have a horrible credit report," she emailed. "I missed two months of credit card payments when Dad died, and the balances are high. [I could] sell the house… but, boy, I hate to move. This farm house is our only stability, as is our neighborhood."

The truth is that there frequently are no easy fixes when you're in a credit crisis. Even solutions that seem like a silver bullet often end up having unintended consequences: on your pocketbook, in your credit score, and in your future financial options.

How you handle credit problems will have a huge effect not only on your credit-worthiness, but also on your financial future. The wrong move can sink you further into debt, devastate what's left of your credit score, and put your entire financial life at risk. The right moves can help you climb out of the hole stronger, wealthier, and more credit-worthy than ever before.

If you're in the midst of a crisis, you'll want to get to work right away to minimize the damage, evaluate your options, and steer your financial ship away from the rocks.

If you've already endured the crisis and are getting back on your feet, you can skip ahead to the next chapter—but you might find some important information here that could help prevent a future catastrophe.

The steps you need to take are fairly straightforward:

1. **Figure out how to free up some cash**—You might not need to tap every source of income you identify, but it's good to know what's available before you go any further.

2. **Evaluate your options**—If you find enough cash, you might be able to set up a repayment plan and put the crisis behind you. If you don't, you have an array of tough but important choices you'll need to consider.

3. **Choose a path and take action**—You might not like all the consequences you'll have to face, but further delay will simply make matters worse. The quicker you pick a plan and get started, the sooner your credit can start to recover.

Before you get started, you'll want some breathing room—psychological "space," if you will—to deal with your financial problems. If you're stressed over bills, give yourself permission to take a deep breath and know that by the end of this process, you'll have a plan. If you and your partner have been fighting over money, you should try to declare a truce while you get things sorted out.

If debt collectors are hounding you, you have the legal right to send them a letter telling them not to contact you, and they're required to comply. You can find a sample letter in Robin Leonard's excellent book *Money Troubles: Legal Strategies to Cope with Your Debts* (2003, Nolo Press).

Unfortunately, some collection agencies have taken to filing lawsuits against consumers who send them such letters. They figure if you won't talk to them on the phone, they'll get your attention by dragging you to court and suing you over your debts. That, of course, can make your current problems even worse.

To avoid having to deal with collectors right now, you might simply want to install caller ID on your phone and screen your calls until you know how you're going to deal with your debts. Do pick up a copy of Leonard's book if collectors are making your life miserable or you're being sued over your debts. I'll try to provide a few suggestions on dealing with collectors in the next two chapters, but this is a complicated area of finance with laws that vary widely across the country. You might well need additional help that is beyond the scope of this book.

Step 1: Figure Out How to Free Up Some Cash

One of the most common mistakes people make in a financial crisis is not cutting back hard enough, fast enough.

Charlie, our animator friend, is a classic example. He knew when his last project ended that hundreds of his fellow animators were out of work and that the next job could be a long time coming. But he hoped for the best. He and his wife even continued paying for their children's private schools; in fact, more than a third of the $150,000 they borrowed went for tuition.

"My wife didn't want to disrupt their lives or their schooling," Charlie explained.

This refusal to cut back is far from unique, according to creditor counselor Steve Rhode, founder of MyVesta.org. People in a financial crisis often put off trimming their budgets, hoping something will come along to save them. That kind of optimistic attitude is perfectly human—and can be perfectly disastrous. It doesn't make much sense to insist that you can't possibly take your kids out of private school only to wind up losing your home.

You might not be paying $50,000 for tuition, but chances are you could find plenty of ways to cut your expenses if you got serious. Perhaps you're clinging to a car you can't afford, an expensive cell phone plan, or a habit of eating out.

If you need help in finding ways to cut costs, check out some of the many frugality-oriented Web sites, such as The Dollar Stretcher at www.stretcher.com or Bankrate.com's Frugal University. You'll find whole shelves of books on this topic at your local library, with Amy Dacyczyn's *Tightwad Gazette* the likely centerpiece.

Or maybe you need to take a hard look at some of your bigger bills. Even your so-called "fixed" expenses, such as your mortgage or rent, aren't really set in stone. Rhode says he often counsels people who struggle to hang on to homes that are simply too expensive for them, when the smarter course would be to move.

Don't panic quite yet. For the moment, you don't have to do anything, other than write down the potential savings you can identify. You might find it helpful to break those savings down into three categories:

- **The easy stuff**—Expenses that you could ditch with little effort

- **The harder stuff**—Expenses that would require more sacrifice to trim

- **The last-ditch stuff**—Expenses you would cut only as a last resort

Again, at this point we're trying to find potential sources of cash so that you can better evaluate your options. Just don't close your mind to what might seem right now like drastic measures.

There are two other good ways to raise cash: by selling stuff and by making more money. If you can sell an extra vehicle, hold a yard sale, or auction unused items on eBay, you might be able to free up a good chunk of change. You also might consider freelance work or a second job temporarily. If you're already working full time, this can seem pretty daunting, but you might be able to do something for a few months that you'd never be able to sustain permanently.

You might notice that I haven't included some of the most-touted "fixes" for credit problems: home equity loans, other debt consolidation loans, and withdrawals or loans from retirement plans. That's because these "solutions," as typically applied, often make matters worse in the long run.

Home equity loans, lines of credit, and cash-out mortgage refinances are particularly seductive, because they tend to offer low rates and tax-deductible interest, to boot. But they come with big problems:

- Most people who use home equity to pay off credit card and other unsecured loans ultimately end up deeper in debt within a few years. That's because they haven't changed the fundamental problem of overspending that got them in trouble in the first place.

- Such loans usually turn what should be short-term debt into long-term debt. You could end up paying more in interest— and again, wind up poorer—than if you'd buckled down and just paid off the cards out of your current income.

- Using these loans to pay off credit cards, medical bills, or personal loans turns unsecured debt, which could have been erased in bankruptcy court, into secured debt that can't be wiped out—and that puts your home at risk as well.

Most retirement plans also are protected from creditors' claims in bankruptcy court and typically shouldn't be used to pay off unsecured debt. In addition, a withdrawal from a 401(k) or IRA means you're losing out on the tax-deferred returns that your money could earn in the plan if you left it alone. Every $10,000 you take out of a 401(k), for example, could cost you $100,000 or more in future retirement income, assuming it had been left alone to grow at an 8 percent average annual rate for 30 years.

The idea that you would protect your retirement or home equity instead of paying debts outrages some people. They feel every possible source of funds should be tapped to pay off debts you owe. If that's the way you feel, fine. But you should remember that the credit card companies are going to thrive whether or not you pay your bills. How will you thrive in retirement if you've decimated your funds before you even get there? Hopefully, your finances will turn out to be healthy enough that you can pay off all your debts, but you should think twice, and then again, before raiding either your retirement or your home.

In addition to the long-term cost, withdrawals from 401(k)s, IRAs, and other plans typically incur heavy penalties and fees. Come April 15, you would face a tax bill equal to 25 percent to 50 percent of what you took out.

Loans from 401(k)s and 403(b)s have their own dangers: If you lose your job, you typically must repay the loan within a few weeks, or you'll owe penalties and taxes on the balance.

Are there exceptions? Of course. You might decide to borrow from your 401(k) to pay the mortgage for a month or two to avoid foreclosure, for example. But if you can't make your house payment any other way than by tapping your retirement funds, you're probably better off selling the place than continuing to struggle only to ultimately lose the property. At least by selling, you can preserve what's left of your equity—and your credit score—so that you'll be in a better position to buy another home when your finances improve.

That's a far better approach than trying to paper over your problem with more loans. Your long-term financial health depends on your fixing these fundamental troubles, not merely delaying the day of reckoning.

As far as debt consolidation loans go, you're almost certainly better off steering clear. There's a lot of consumer abuse, if not outright fraud, in this area. High, hidden fees are common, as are loans that just stretch out your obligation and ultimately cost you more than if you'd paid off the original debt.

The same goes for debt settlement firms. These outfits promise to settle your debts for pennies on the dollar—often, supposedly, without hurting your credit. In reality, debt settlement tactics often leave your credit score in shreds, and sometimes the company simply disappears with your big up-front fee.

And don't get me started about "debt elimination" firms, which use cockamamie theories about the Declaration of Independence or "natural law" to argue that you don't really owe what you owe.

If you really can't pay all of your unsecured debts, your best bet usually is to file for bankruptcy rather than messing with half measures. You can get a fresh start, and you'll have the money you otherwise would have thrown at these non-starter "solutions."

But before you take that drastic step, you need to know more about your choices.

Step 2: Evaluating Your Options

This step actually includes a number of other tasks, all of which take a little time, but are essential to making sure you choose the right option.

Task 1: Prioritize Your Bills

If you're being hounded by creditors or are simply stressed by debt, it can be easy for your priorities to get out of whack. You might wind up paying a credit card bill when the rent or mortgage is due just because a collection agency is making your life miserable. You'd be risking eviction or foreclosure over a bill that could be wiped out in bankruptcy court, or at least postponed without major consequences.

That's why it's so important to get creditors off your back with the letter I mentioned earlier. *You* need to be the one deciding how your bills get paid without undue outside pressure.

Once again, we'll be dividing into threes: essential bills, important bills, and non-essential bills.

Essential bills are the ones that, if you didn't pay, would result in catastrophic consequences.

The Bill	The Consequence for Not Paying
Mortgage or rent	Foreclosure or eviction
Home equity loans or lines of credit	Foreclosure or eviction
Groceries	Starvation
Utilities	Absence of lights, heat, water, or phone
Payments on a car needed for work	Lost job
Essential medical treatments	Death or serious illness
Child support	Jail

Important bills are the ones that you should pay if at all possible, because failure to pay them would have serious consequences. Here are some examples.

The Bill	The Potential Consequence
Income taxes	Wage garnishment, loss of tax refund
Court judgments	Wage garnishment
Student loans	Wage garnishment, loss of tax refund
Loans secured by property you want to keep	Repossession of property
Auto insurance	Loss of license, fine
Medical insurance	Catastrophic medical bills

Nonessential bills include debts that aren't secured by property. Failure to pay these debts could have serious repercussions for your credit score and might eventually result in lawsuits and judgments. But skipping the payments listed below won't put you out on the street.

Bills To Pay On Time

Credit cards

Department store cards

Gas cards

Medical bills

Legal bills

Personal loans

Loans from friends or family members

You might have other bills not mentioned here; use your best judgment to categorize them.

After you have your list, go back and add two more columns:

- The monthly payment you typically make

- The minimum monthly payment you need to make to stay current

The minimum for most "friends and family" loans, by the way, is zero—unless you borrowed from your Uncle Tony, and his last name is Soprano.

Task 2: Match Your Resources to Your Bills and Debts

Look at the first two categories of savings that you identified in step 1—the easy stuff to cut, and the harder stuff—and then add those to your monthly net income (what you get in your paycheck after all the taxes and other deductions have been taken). Now compare that income to your first two priorities—essential bills and important bills. Can you cover the minimums required?

If not, you might have some options before opting for the last-ditch cost-cutting measures. It's frequently possible, for example, to get forbearance on your student loans or negotiate payment plans with the IRS. The first you can do yourself, just by talking to your lender; for IRS help, you're probably best off using a tax pro. Even child support can be reduced if you prove to the court that your financial situation has worsened, but this can take awhile and might require a lawyer's help.

Other possibilities: You might take that second job we talked about earlier. You could increase your paycheck by eliminating or reducing 401(k) contributions temporarily or, if you get a tax refund, by reducing your withholding.

If you still can't pay for the essential and the important, you'll probably need to take some last-resort action, such as selling a house if you own one or renting cheaper digs. You'll also need to consult a bankruptcy attorney about wiping out any nonessential debts, because those obviously aren't going to get paid.

If you have your bases covered and have money left over, however, check to see if you can pay the minimums on your nonessential bills. If you can pay at least that much, you're ready for the next task.

Task 3: Figuring Out a Repayment Plan

Your mission: To see if you can pay off those nonessential debts, other than friends and family loans, in three to five years.

Why that particular time period?

Because that's the standard generally used in bankruptcy court. If you have enough income and assets to pay most or all of your bills within that time frame, a judge probably wouldn't let you pursue a Chapter 7 bankruptcy.

There's a dandy free tool at the Quicken.com Web site called the Debt Reduction Planner. With it you can experiment to see how long it might take you to pay off your unsecured debts. Similar tools are available in personal finance software, such as Quicken and Money. Don't include your mortgage, student loans, or any other "essential" or "important" bills we covered in the previous task; you're just trying to design a plan for those nonessential debts.

First see how much progress you can make with the increased income you identified; then add in the lump sums you've estimated that you could raise by selling stuff. Finally, check out how fast you could get out of debt if you took some of those last-ditch options.

You also could consider—carefully—using a home equity loan or line of credit to pay off your cards. But do so only if you can commit to the following:

- Not using your credit cards to pile up more debt. (For most people, this will mean not using cards at all until the home equity borrowing is paid back.)

- Not borrowing more than 90 percent of your home equity (and preferably less than 80 percent) when your mortgage and home equity borrowing is combined. Home equity can be an important source of emergency funds that you don't want to squander.

- Paying off the debt in the same three- to five-year period. In other words, don't use the home equity loan as an excuse to stretch out your debt.

Remember: If you don't commit to these steps, you'll ultimately just drive yourself deeper into debt.

In the best-case scenario, you'd be able to retire your credit card and other unsecured debt in less than five years without too much strain. If you still have good credit scores, you might even be able to convince your lenders—just by asking—to lower your interest rate so that you can get the debt paid off faster. Credit card companies are often eager to give their best customers a break, rather than risk losing them to competitors.

Of course, that particular door might be closed to you if you've already fallen behind on your payments. Late payments to even one of your creditors can cause the others to raise their interest rates and get tougher about terms. Most credit card companies today periodically check your credit report and, as soon as they notice trouble on any of your accounts, take punitive action. They might jack up your rates by 10 percentage points or more, or quickly lower your credit limits so that you start racking up "over limit" fees. All this can make it that much harder to try to get your head above water.

If things are bad when you're just late with a few payments, you can imagine how lenders—and your credit scores—react when an account is unpaid for so long that the original creditor "charges off" the account. A charge-off is an accounting term that means the lender has given up hope of collecting. Accounts are typically charged off if they're unpaid for six months. Although some creditors then turn the account over to their internal collections departments, others sell the account for pennies on the dollar to outside collection firms.

Interestingly, it's the charge-off itself that does the most damage to your score. Collection actions are serious as well, but what matters most is what the original creditor says about your account—and a charge-off is pretty much the worst thing the creditor can say.

If you're in this situation, consult Leonard's book for a detailed summary of your rights as well as the best strategies for negotiating with collection agencies. The fine points of dealing with collectors are well beyond the scope of this book.

But, as far as your credit score is concerned, you should keep these points in mind:

- Although late payments can really hurt a credit score, a charge-off is even worse. If at all possible, you should try to avoid letting an account lapse for so long that it's charged off.

- If an account has not yet been charged off, try to pay the balance in full either at once or over time. Settling the account with the original creditor for less than you owe can really hurt your credit score. (Settlements on collection accounts typically don't have as negative an effect; see the next chapter for details.)

- If an account has been sent to collections, you'll have the most leverage to negotiate if you can pay a lump sum. But even if you have to make payments, try to negotiate to have the collection action deleted from your credit report if at all possible. Although having the collection deleted won't erase the negative marks from your file—the most damaging mark is the charge-off, which the original creditor typically won't drop—getting rid of the collection notation often helps your score.

What if you can't find a way to get all your unsecured debts paid off, or you're simply not sure if your plan will work? You essentially have two options: credit counseling or bankruptcy. Read on for what you need to know about each.

The Real Scoop on Credit Counseling

You've probably seen the ads on television, the radio, and the Internet promising to "lower your interest rates," "reduce your monthly payments," "end collection calls," and "get you on the road to financial freedom."

Sometimes credit counseling agencies deliver on their promises. Other times, consumers wind up much worse off. Just read what Jeff in Cincinnati went through:

"A little over five years ago, I contacted AmeriDebt to see if they could lower the interest rates on my credit cards. Within 30 minutes, I had received a callback from a representative from AmeriDebt stating that they had lowered the rates on my credit cards. I was amazed at the speed in which they had done this. I started paying them $500 a month, and they were to disburse the funds to my creditors. The problem was they never paid my creditors. [After five months], they had $2,500 of my money that the creditors should have received. This sent my credit into a tailspin. I was not in trouble with my creditors and had never missed a payment of any kind until I started dealing with [this company]. The credit card companies were calling, and they stated that they had no record of AmeriDebt working on my behalf. Bottom line: My credit was now ruined. I went from a 750 Beacon score to a 520 within four months. I paid everyone off immediately, and it has taken almost five years to get my credit score to just below 700. The funny part is that AmeriDebt decided to finally pay out that $2,500 to my creditors after I [had] already paid them off."

AmeriDebt insisted that it helped hundreds of thousands of consumers pay their bills and avoid bankruptcy. It continued insisting, in fact, right up until the Federal Trade Commission sued the company in 2003. The FTC said AmeriDebt lied to its customers about the fees it charged and the services it offered, leaving many of them worse off.

What's more, regulators said, AmeriDebt posed as a nonprofit company while actually funneling money to a for-profit arm.

AmeriDebt responded by closing its doors to new customers—but sending them to another heavily advertised credit counselor making similar claims of quick-and-easy solutions to debt problems.

Credit counseling used to be a sleepy field dominated by the National Foundation for Credit Counseling, a truly nonprofit organization that was funded in large part by contributions from banks and credit card companies. Its mission was to negotiate lower interest rates and payments for cash-strapped consumers so that they could avoid bankruptcy. The lender receiving these payments would return a portion of each check—a contribution known as "fair share"—to the credit-counseling agency to fund its operations.

As consumer debt spiraled in the 1990s, however, a new breed of credit counselor emerged, eager to get a piece of those lender contributions. To boost market share, these new counselors started going after customers who were perfectly able to make their payments but who just wanted a lower interest rate.

Disgusted, the major creditors started dropping their "fair share" contributions, making it tougher for the older agencies to make ends meet. Instead of supporting legitimate counselors, some credit card companies even tried to steer consumers away from counseling, telling them erroneously that such help was as bad for their credit as bankruptcy.

But that wasn't the worst of it. Many of the new credit counselors kept the first month's contributions or charged other fat, hidden fees. Some failed to pass along consumers' contributions at all, causing multiple late payments that devastated scores. Former employees of such firms told Congress that they were forced to use fake names and employ high-pressure "boiler room" tactics to sign up new customers. The emphasis was on collecting fees—not providing counseling or offering education that might help consumers understand how to avoid debt in the future.

The fact that there are so many bad guys out there shouldn't make you avoid credit counseling entirely if you could benefit from legitimate help. If you're already behind on your bills, unable to make minimum payments, borrowing from one card to pay another, or otherwise demonstrating signs of extreme financial distress, credit counseling might be preferable to bankruptcy.

Credit counseling is not a good option if you're current on your bills and able to pay more than the minimums. As I explained in a previous chapter, credit counseling itself won't hurt your credit score, but the reactions of some of your lenders might.

In short, you need to tread carefully. Here are some of the things you need to consider before signing up with a credit counselor:

- **Is it accredited?** You'll want a counselor affiliated with the National Foundation for Credit Counseling or the Association of Independent Consumer Credit Counseling Agencies. You can find affiliated agencies at www.nfcc.org or www.aiccca.org, respectively.

- **What do regulators say about it?** At a minimum, make two calls: one to your local Better Business Bureau and one to your state attorney general's office. Ask how many complaints have been made about the agency and see if any regulatory actions are pending against them.

- **What does the agency say about its services?** Avoid an outfit that says credit counseling will have no negative impact on your credit or one that promises to settle your debts for less than you owe without affecting your credit. Such unrealistic promises are a clear sign that you're not dealing with a legitimate operator.

- **What fees are involved?** Legitimate credit counselors have had to raise their fees in recent years, but if you're paying much more than $50 to set up your plan, you're probably paying too much.

- **When and how much will creditors get paid?** You know that missing or late payments can devastate your credit score. Make sure the counselor tells you, preferably in writing, how much of each monthly payment you make will go directly to your creditors and when the payments will arrive.

It's possible that after all this investigation, you'll discover that a credit counselor's debt management plan won't work. If your credit counselor crunches the numbers and discovers the agency can't help you pay off your bills within five years, you'll probably be told to "explore other legal options." That's code for: Talk to a bankruptcy attorney.

You might want to do that anyway, just to get more information about your options before you decide on a plan. Such a consultation is particularly important if your debts are overwhelming and you have equity in a home. States treat this equity differently, with some protecting all or most of it in bankruptcy court and others figuring it's up for grabs. If you can't protect your equity, it might be worth getting a home equity loan to pay off your debts, assuming you have enough equity available.

After you've heard what both the credit counselor and the bankruptcy attorney have to say, you can weigh all the information you've been given and make a choice.

Should You File for Bankruptcy?

In the fall of 2003, I asked MSN readers to share their bankruptcy stories—why they filed, how it has affected them, and whether they thought they made the right choice. I expected a few dozen replies.

I received more than 500 before my email box overloaded and stopped accepting new messages. I was stunned not only at the breadth of the response, but the depth. Most were long, detailed missives that recounted financial catastrophes, such as lost jobs and huge medical bills, personal tragedies including the death of a spouse or a child, and a wide variety of human miscalculations: trusting the wrong business partner, marrying a secret gambler, or simply spending way more than they earned.

Most believed that filing bankruptcy was the right choice for them, although many admitted to mixed feelings. Here's just a small cross-section of their responses:

> *"I filed last year and released about... $40,000 in credit card debt. I researched and pondered the idea for quite awhile before actually doing it, but ultimately it provided me a fresh start. Now I am a regular, financially upstanding citizen, and I have learned my lesson... Had I not been protected by bankruptcy laws, I would still be struggling."*
> *—Erin in Honolulu*

"I don't think bankruptcy is ever the 'right' decision, but I felt it was my only choice at the time. For me, it was embarrassing and humiliating... It is now six years later, and I've done all I can to restore my credit by making sure all my bills are paid on time, and I pay all my debts as quickly as possible. The children are both now grown and on their own, I'm making twice the wages I was [at the time of the filing]... that doesn't make any difference. I still have trouble getting credit."
—*Cathy in Montana*

"I filed bankruptcy in 1998 and have gotten myself in trouble once again. Currently I'm about $3,000 in debt, which consists of cell phone bills and credit cards that started out with a limit of $300 or $500... all of which are probably in or close to being in collection."
—*Leslie in Washington, D.C.*

"We filed Chap. 7 in 1999 due to bills piling up as a result of [our business failing]. One year later, we applied and were approved for a credit card with a 13 percent interest rate. I also bought a new car at what I consider a somewhat outrageous rate of 16 percent and missed out on all the 0 percent financing offered after Sept. 11. Basically, one can survive a bankruptcy as long as the pay history is kept up to date on all debts afterward."
—*Rob in Grand Prairie, Texas*

"It has been almost four years since I sat in an attorney's office, papers filled in ready to file for bankruptcy. I was a newly sober alcoholic wanting to make a fresh start in my new life... I decided that filing for bankruptcy was a cop-out, and that it was unfair to the companies (small and large) that I had defaulted on. Since that day, I have [been making payments]... In April of 2007, my record will be clear of all negative items, and I achieved this without filing bankruptcy."
Ken in Santa Rosa, California

As you can see from these responses, people's experiences with bankruptcy can vary widely. Whether or not it's the right choice depends on the types of debt you owe and the amounts; your income and resources; and your ability to navigate the inevitable fall-out, among other factors.

The Type of Bankruptcy You File Matters

The majority of people who file for bankruptcy opt for Chapter 7, which wipes out most unsecured debts. (Unsecured debts are those that aren't linked to specific property, such as a car or a house. So your mortgage is a secured debt; your credit card bills are unsecured.)

Filing a Chapter 7 bankruptcy can mean you have to give up some of your assets (property or cash) to pay your creditors. In reality, most Chapter 7 filers aren't required to give up anything, either because they don't have any assets or because the property they have is "exempt" or protected from creditors. The exemptions vary by state, but they might include household furnishings, clothing, tools you need for work, retirement accounts, and some—or all—of the equity in your home.

If you want to keep property that isn't exempt, you can still file for bankruptcy, but you typically must choose Chapter 13. Chapter 13 requires debtors to come up with a plan to repay all, or most, of their debts within five years. If they successfully complete their plan, they're allowed to keep their property while having any remaining debts erased. Unfortunately, most people fail to complete their Chapter 13 plans, and their cases are either dismissed, allowing creditors to resume collection activities, or converted to Chapter 7s.

A bankruptcy filing can make sense if any of the following apply:

- You can't pay back most or all of your unsecured debts in three to five years.

- You don't have much equity in a home or vehicle or much other property to speak of.

- You *do* have considerable equity in a home or vehicle or other valuables that wouldn't be exempt in bankruptcy—jewels; family heirlooms; valuable artwork or collections; or stocks, bonds, and cash held outside a retirement plan—but you're willing to agree to a Chapter 13 repayment plan rather than a Chapter 7 liquidation.

Bankruptcy might not make sense if any of these apply:

- You could repay your debts within five years.

- Most of your debts are the kind that can't be wiped out. Debts that typically can't be erased include student loans, child support, and recent taxes. You might still decide to file so that you can free up more money for these debts, but the disadvantages of filing might well overwhelm the advantages.

- You defrauded your creditors by hiding assets, say, or lying about your income or debts on a credit application.

- You recently ran up large debts buying luxuries, which can include vacations and entertainment. If you did so while you were clearly broke, that can constitute fraud. If you ran up the bills and then lost your job, you might be able to file for bankruptcy on other debts, but the luxury debts might not be wiped out.

- You want to file a Chapter 7 liquidation bankruptcy and received a discharge for a previous bankruptcy filing within the past six years. (You can file for a Chapter 13 repayment plan bankruptcy at any time.)

- You're reluctant to leave a coborrower solely responsible for a debt. A bankruptcy filing can wipe out your legal obligation to repay a loan, but creditors can still go after a cosigner or joint borrower.

Making the decision to file isn't an easy one, and you'd be smart to get expert help to explore your options.

Step 3: Choose Your Path and Take Action

When faced with unappealing choices, it's natural to procrastinate. But after you've assessed your situation, gathered the relevant information, and sought expert help, the path you need to take should be pretty clear.

Option 1: The Pay-Off Plan

If you can pay off your unsecured debts without help or with the help of home equity borrowing, you're ready to take the first step: cutting up your credit cards. "What?" you might be saying. "Cut up my cards? How can I live without my cards?" News flash: People do it all the time.

You can't get out of debt if you keep digging. And if you have easy access to your cards, you'll keep using them. Your credit cards need to be off limits until you're debt free. Debit cards with Visa or MasterCard logos are accepted at most places that take credit cards; the difference is that the money comes directly out of your checking account, so it's much tougher to overspend.

You don't need to actually close your credit card accounts, which could potentially hurt your score, unless you really have an uncontrollable spending issue.

Next, set up an automatic payment plan as outlined earlier to pay off your debts. The order in which you pay them depends on your particular situation. If you have an account that's close to being charged off, for example, you'll probably want to catch up with that one right away while paying the minimums on your other debts. If you're not behind, you could start paying down the account that's closest to its limit, or the one that's charging the highest nondeductible interest rate. After the first debt is retired, redirect the biggest payment to the next highest-rate—or closest-to-the-limit—debt. Continue this pattern until all the debts are retired.

Option 2: Credit Counseling

If you decide you need a credit counselor's aid, make the appointment to get started on a debt management plan. Every day you delay is costing you more in interest and putting off the moment when you'll be debt free.

Understand that paying off your debts will be a long-term commitment, and that living on the tight budget necessary may be frustrating. If you need motivation to keep going, consider joining the message boards of one of the frugality-oriented Web sites to get support and keep your spirits up.

Option 3: Bankruptcy

If bankruptcy is the best of bad options, then file. The bankruptcy laws were designed to give people a fresh start, and if you've done your best to find money to pay your bills and failed, you shouldn't shun this option.

6

REBUILDING YOUR SCORE AFTER A CREDIT DISASTER

So you've weathered the financial storm. Now what do you do about the mess that was left behind?

Your credit file might be littered with delinquencies, collection actions, repossessions, or even bankruptcy. You might worry that these mistakes will haunt you forever, or at least make getting credit terribly difficult and expensive.

Some people are so frustrated with their bad credit that they simply give up. Maureen in Cleveland wrote me about her daughter and son-in-law, who were turned down for several loans after filing bankruptcy. Humiliated, they vowed never to approach another lender.

"They've given up on their dream of owning their own house someday,"
Maureen wrote. "I know they could do something about their credit if
they would just try."

Contrast their attitude with that of Chance, an Indiana loan officer who filed for Chapter 7 bankruptcy five years earlier at age 26.

"Today I have a 697 middle score and I can get a loan for anything I want to," Chance wrote. "I own a home and two rental properties, have a brand new auto and motorcycle . . . Being in the mortgage industry, I knew I could overcome the bankruptcy, because I knew how the credit system worked."

How quickly you can recover from your past credit mistakes depends largely on you—and what you do now. If, like Chance, you understand how the system works, you can minimize the length of time you spend in the credit penalty box.

You can start putting the past behind you immediately. Credit scoring formulas care more about what you've done recently than what you've done in the past, so making the right moves now can set you on the path to good credit.

You won't be able to erase your mistakes overnight. However, most people with past credit problems can achieve a substantial boost in their credit scores within a couple of years. By the time the last negative item drops off your credit report—after seven years for most black marks, or up to 10 for a Chapter 7 bankruptcy—you could have a credit score that's actually better than average.

Part I: Credit Report Repair

Many people who have credit problems are terrified at the prospect of looking at their credit report. It's the same dread they might have felt as children about a bad report card, only amplified by their adult knowledge of how destructive poor credit can be.

In actuality, your report might be better than you think. Some of the problems you are worried about might never have been reported to the credit bureaus, or they might have less of an effect than you fear.

On the other hand, your credit file might be a bit of a nightmare, with every slipup documented in black and white. Your report might even make your problems look worse than they actually were. It's not uncommon to have two or more collections reported for the same debt, for example, or for other errors to creep in that can really hammer your credit score.

You might, for example, be the victim of an unscrupulous collection agency that has illegally "re-aged" a debt—in other words, reported the account to the credit bureaus in a way that makes your mistake look more recent than it actually is. Beth in Los Angeles wrote about just such a scofflaw:

"My husband and I had a dispute with a cable company over a box that they never gave us, but that they claimed we owed $200 for when we closed the account before we moved. To make a long story short, the item ended up on our credit report as a collection account.

"We waited anxiously for that to roll off of our report. At the six-year, two month mark, another collection agency called us. They said they had bought the account, and that the seven-year 'clock' started again when they bought it. They said unless we paid them, they would report it as a new debt and it would remain on our credit report for seven more years."

The good news is that you're not helpless. There are steps you can take to clean up your credit, chase off mistakes, fight back against illegal tactics, and even—perhaps—scoot some of those bad marks off your report without having to wait for the usual 7- or 10-year period to expire.

Scrutinize Your Report For Serious Errors

Your first move, obviously, is to get copies of your credit reports from all three bureaus, using the addresses or Web sites listed in Chapter 3,"Improving Your Score—the Right Way." Make sure you get three separate reports, rather than a "3-in-1" or "tri-merged" report that combines information from the three bureaus. Although these merged reports are helpful to lenders, they might not include all of the information that's included in each of the individual bureaus' files.

Follow the steps listed in Chapter 3 for reviewing your report, noting any problems for dispute with the respective credit bureaus. Look especially for the following:

- Delinquencies that are older than seven years, or accounts listed as delinquent that don't include the date of delinquency

- Bankruptcies that are older than 10 years or that aren't listed by the specific chapter

- Judgments or paid liens older than seven years

- Paid-off debts listed as unpaid

- Accounts that were wiped up by a bankruptcy filing still listed as "past due" instead of as "included in bankruptcy"

- More than one collection account for the same debt

- Collection accounts that don't show the date that the original account went delinquent

- Any accounts, delinquencies, collections, and so on that aren't yours

When it's time to actually dispute the errors you find, you have a choice about whether to make your beefs online or by snail mail. Some credit repair veterans prefer to use the online dispute process that's available when you get your reports via the Web; they believe there's less likelihood of their disputes getting "lost" because the electronic process typically dumps their complaints directly into the bureaus' computer systems. If you do opt for online disputes, make printouts of every form you fill out and every response you get. Doing so establishes the kind of paper trail that can be incredibly helpful if you run into problems.

The need for a paper trail is why others insist that all communication with bureaus, creditors, and especially collection agencies should be in writing and sent certified mail, return receipt requested. Keep the little green cards you get back, along with copies of the letters and any documentation you might submit. Because you're probably new to the credit repair process, you might want to start out doing things the old-fashioned way and switch to the electronic process only when you become more comfortable with the system.

Know Your Rights

Before you dispute anything, though, you need to know your rights under the Fair Credit Reporting Act. They are as follows:

- **The right to have your dispute investigated.** The bureaus must investigate your dispute, usually within 30 days, by contacting the creditor, collection agency, or other "information provider" that supplied the data that is in question. Any information provider contacted in this way must launch its own investigation and report its results back to the bureau.

  There's a major exception to the 30-day rule. If the credit bureaus decide your dispute is "frivolous," they might tell you so and refuse to investigate. This tends to happen if you repeatedly demand investigations of information that's already been verified. Although this can prevent scam artists from taking advantage of the system, it can be frustrating for people who are dealing with a creditor that refuses to correct its errors. I'll discuss strategies in the section, "What to Do If a Credit Bureau Won't Budge."

- **The right to have erroneous information corrected.** If the provider says the information is indeed inaccurate, it is required to notify not just the bureau that originally contacted it, but all the other major credit bureaus as well so that the error can be fixed or the item deleted. If the provider can't verify the information, the information must be deleted from your credit report.

  The bureaus can, however, reinsert the deleted information or undo the correction down the road if the provider later verifies that the original item was in fact complete and correct. This exception can frustrate the heck out of consumers who think they have their reports cleaned up, only to see the bad information pop up again after a few months.

- **The right to a written response.** After completing its investigation, the bureau must give you a written report of its findings and a free copy of your credit report if the investigation changed anything on your file.

  Furthermore, if the bureau later restores the information that was deleted or changed, it must notify you in writing and provide you with the name, address, and phone number of the information provider.

- **The right to have a statement included in your file.** If the dispute doesn't resolve the way you want, you are entitled to a 100-word statement inserted into your credit report explaining your side of the story.

  As you read in the last chapter, though, these statements have no effect on a credit score. Therefore, even though you have this right, you're far better off pursuing other avenues that can actually make a difference if you're being stymied by a recalcitrant creditor.

- **The right to sue**. If a creditor or collection agency violates these rights—by continuing to report inaccurate, unsubstantiated information, for example, or failing to respond to your dispute—you can sue the creditor or agency in state or federal court. Some people have even pursued these claims successfully in small claims court.

  Hopefully, your problems can be resolved without a judge's involvement. But you might need the threat of a lawsuit, and perhaps legal representation to back it up, if you're dealing with a particularly troublesome creditor or unresponsive credit bureau.

Organize Your Attack

At this point, you should divide the errors you've discovered into two groups. The first group includes unpaid debts that actually belong to you (as opposed to debts that you didn't incur or that belong to someone else), including any debt you suspect was illegally re-aged, and any collection accounts (whether they're legitimately yours or not). All the other errors you discover—accounts that aren't yours, old delinquencies on paid-up accounts, debts that were included in bankruptcy but aren't listed that way, and so on—should be included in the second group.

You can get started disputing the items in that second group right away. Include copies of any documentation you have that supports your assertion with your letters to the credit bureaus. (Never send originals.) After you've notified the credit bureaus, follow up by sending a letter (certified, return receipt requested) to the creditor that supplied the erroneous information. Now the creditors and the bureaus are all on notice that there's a problem. Failure to act on their part would be a violation of the FCRA and grounds enough for a lawsuit—again, if it comes to that.

In many cases, the creditors and bureaus will correct legitimate errors. However, you'll still need to monitor your credit reports to make sure the bad information doesn't pop up again in the future. If that happens, the paperwork you've kept—including notification that the bureaus give you about the changes they've made—might help you get the errors removed more quickly.

If the creditor or other information provider insists that its information is accurate, however, you might need to dispute the information with them again—or you might just want to head straight to a lawyer. Sometimes a firmly worded missive on an attorney's letterhead is all it takes to get a creditor to see the errors of its ways. If not, there's always a lawsuit.

The National Association of Consumer Advocates at www.naca.net can provide referrals to attorneys. You also can check out one of the many Web sites devoted to do-it-yourself credit repair, such as CreditBoards.com, for help in researching these issues or even pursuing a lawsuit on your own. These sites, in which consumers exchange information with each other, can be incredibly helpful to the beginner, but might also include erroneous information and are no substitute for real legal advice. If you do choose to use such a site, plan to spend several hours reading the "frequently asked questions" sections and learning the protocol for asking questions before posting for the first time.

What You Need to Know About Unpaid Debts and Collections

Now let's return to that first group of errors you identified—the ones dealing with collection accounts and valid, unpaid debts. These were segregated, because different rules apply.

When it comes to collections, you have another important right as outlined in the Fair Debt Collection Practices Act:

- **The right to have a collection account "validated."** This process, as outlined in the FDCPA, is quite different from the "verification" process referred to above. When a credit bureau asks a creditor to "verify" information, the investigation that follows can be pretty cursory. The creditor reviews its records and any information supplied by the consumer and then decides whether it (the creditor) was right or wrong.

  When a collection agency is asked to validate a debt, by contrast, the process can get pretty involved. The collector must *prove* that the debt is your responsibility, and also that they have the legal right to collect it from you. Furthermore, the collector has to cease all collection activity until they provide this evidence to you. If the agency can't validate the debt, it must end its attempts to collect on the debt and stop reporting the collections account to the credit bureaus.

Note that your right to validation applies specifically to collection agencies, not to the original creditor. Collection agency records are presumed to be less reliable than those kept by the original creditors. Collectors are often guilty of going after the wrong people or misstating the amounts owed; the validation process is meant to protect consumers from those practices.

To validate a debt, the collector needs to present documentation—obtained from the original creditor—proving that you do indeed owe the money.

Validation can be a powerful weapon in your fight to clean up collection actions on your credit report. Many times collectors don't have the documentation required, especially if the debt has been passed around from one collection agency to another, as often happens. Frequently, they have little more than a computer printout to back up their claims, and the Federal Trade Commission has made it clear that such a "mere itemization" isn't sufficient proof to constitute a validation of a debt.

The validation process can not only help you eliminate collection accounts that don't belong to you, but it might help you get rid of some that actually do.

That last statement might surprise you, particularly if you've heard the credit bureau company line that you can't legally remove true, negative information from your credit report. I admit that I used to parrot that line myself, usually when trying to warn people away from the many scam artists who promise to erase all of the bad information on your credit report in exchange for a fat fee.

I've since learned that sometimes—not always, but sometimes—you *can* get accurate information removed from your file, especially if it has to do with an old collection account.

Now, the bureaus and Fair Isaac will tell you that this isn't "playing fair"—that the integrity of the credit system depends on credit reports reflecting the most complete picture possible, including all available negative and positive information.

Unfortunately, the bureaus are still allowing far too much erroneous data to seep into their system, and that's hurting consumers. The credit-reporting process is still weighted heavily in favor of lenders and collectors.

That steams Jim Stephenson, a Realtor in Branson, Missouri, who has watched several of his clients struggle with inaccurate credit information:

> *"If I'm a subscriber [to the credit bureaus], all I need is your Social Security number and I can tell them anything derogatory about you I want. Without question or hesitation, this info goes onto your credit file. It can be extremely difficult to prove a negative. How do you prove that you don't owe me money?" Jim wrote. "Time and again I have witnessed firsthand the inability of a client to have misinformation that is irrefutably not my client's debt removed without a protracted and costly fight. Why is this? It's because the burden of proof is on the accused, not the accuser."*

The issue of re-aging can be particularly troublesome. The 7-year limit on reporting most negative items was designed to give consumers some protection against relentless creditors. In effect, lawmakers were trying to prevent collection agencies from creating a sort of perpetual debtors' prison for people who had made mistakes. Congress even strengthened the law in the mid-1990s to prevent collectors from endlessly extending the 7-year period time just by passing an account from one agency to the next (as Beth's collection agency was threatening to do). Instead of using the "date of last activity," as was common before 1997, the 7-year clock now starts 180 days after the account first became delinquent.

To get around the limit, some collection agencies are now simply flout-ing the law and pretending an old debt is a new one. I've received numerous letters from consumers who had long-forgotten delinquent accounts suddenly pop back up on their credit reports with a new and phony date. One of the largest collection agencies, NCO Financial Systems, agreed in early 2004 to settle a lawsuit with a group of borrowers over this very issue.

Unfortunately, the type of collector that would actually post false infor-mation to a credit bureau file might not be the type that will back down in the face of a validation demand or a credit bureau investigation. You'll still need to make the validation demand, of course, and follow up with a credit bureau dispute if you don't get the response you want. But it might take a lawsuit to get the falsely incriminating information out of your file.

There's another issue. Plenty of consumers are like Beth and Dave in Chapter 5 in that they let a spat with a merchant get out of hand and wound up with collections on their reports. These collections—even for small amounts—can have an outsized effect on a credit score. The thinner or younger your credit file, the worse a collection can hurt. Although mortgage lenders tend to ignore these small accounts, the credit scoring formula most emphatically does not. Getting rid of collections can create a more accurate picture of your credit habits.

It's also not uncommon to have two, three, or even more collection accounts reported for the same debt. That amplifies the damage to your credit score and reflects the collection industry's practice of selling and reselling the same debt to different companies. Weeding out some of these extraneous collection accounts provides a more accurate picture of your credit situation.

Besides, I'm going to assume that if you care enough about your credit to read this book and spend the time necessary to clean up your credit report, you're demonstrating the kind of dedication and responsibility that should make you a good credit risk in the future.

You shouldn't assume, however, that you can get every piece of negative information removed—far from it. The more recent the negative mark, the less likely you'll get it to budge. Your chances of success will improve as the "sin" gets older.

You also have no guarantee that getting rid of a collection action will help your score much if at all. The scoring formula generally weighs what the original creditor had to say about you more heavily than what any subsequent collector reports. In other words, delinquencies and charge-offs reported by the original creditor can still hurt your score even if the subsequent collec-tion(s) disappear.

Okay, that's enough background. If you're trying to get rid of a collection action, credit repair veterans suggest first disputing it as "not mine," rather than starting off with a validation demand.

Sometimes, the collection agency simply won't bother to verify the account, particularly if it's old or small. If that's the case, the collection will be dropped from your report—no muss, no fuss.

If the credit bureau verifies the account, go directly to the collection agency and demand validation. You can find sample letters at Web sites such as CreditBoards.com, CreditInfoCenter.com, or CreditInsider.com. Essentially, you need to tell the collection agency that under the Fair Debt Collection Practices Act, it must prove that you owe this debt. Demand copies of documents such as the signed account agreement that created the debt and the agreement with the original creditor that gives the agency the right to try to collect the debt.

If the collector fails to respond or can't provide sufficient evidence that you owe the debt, it's supposed to remove the collection from your report. If that doesn't happen, you can bring the matter to the attention of the credit bureaus and ask for reinvestigations. Make sure you make it clear to the bureaus that this is not a repeat of your earlier request; provide the evidence that you asked for validation, and let them know that the collector didn't comply.

If the account doesn't disappear at this point, you have both the bureaus and the collection agency on the hook for credit-reporting violations and potentially could pursue a lawsuit.

What You Need to Know About Statutes of Limitations

Before we go any further down this path, however, you need to know about one more factor that will affect your credit repair efforts: statutes of limitations.

You already know that credit bureaus have a limited time (7 to 10 years) in which they can report negative information. The statutes of limitations I'm talking about, however, curb the amount of time that a creditor can sue you over a debt.

Statutes of limitations vary widely by state and might depend on the type of debt involved. In Alaska, for example, creditors can't sue you after three years have passed since the delinquency. In Kentucky, the statute is 15 years for written contracts, and 5 for oral contracts. Depending on the state, open-ended contracts—such as credit cards—might be considered a written contract, an oral contract, or have a different statute of limitations altogether.

That's not the end of the complexities and vagaries. What if you incurred the debt in one state but now live in another? Typically, it's the state you live in now that matters, but not always.

Also, you can restart an expired statute of limitations in some states by making a payment on an old debt, or just by acknowledging that you owe the money.

Now, you don't have to worry about any of this if the item you're trying to get deleted is a paid collection and is listed that way on your credit report. If it's an unpaid collection, or any unpaid account for that matter, you'll want to do some legal research to make sure that you understand the statutes that apply in your situation:

- If a debt is still within the statute of limitations and it's actually your debt, you want to be careful about disputing the information with the credit bureaus. Remember the phrase, "Let sleeping dogs lie?" You could reawaken interest in collecting the debt by drawing it to the creditor's attention. If you're not prepared to pay the debt or get sued and suffer the potential ding to your credit score that either action could evoke, the better course might be to leave the debt alone and hope it slides silently off your credit report in a few years. (See the later section "Should You Pay Old Debts" for more details.)

- If the statute of limitations is well past, you can be more aggressive in trying to get an old debt off your report. If you choose this course, though, make sure you don't do anything that could start the statute of limitations all over again.

  If you're unwilling to handle all this yourself—and it is a lot to expect a layperson to do—a few good law firms handle cases like this. Use the National Association of Consumer Advocates to get a referral, though, and steer clear of any law firm or other outfit that guarantees results or demands enormous fees in advance.

Should You Pay Old Debts?

Legally, you owe a debt until it's paid, settled, or wiped out in bankruptcy.

Some people erroneously believe that their obligation ends when a creditor charges off the debt. But a charge-off is essentially just an accounting term. The creditor can continue trying to collect or sell the debt to a collection agency, which can try to get you to pay.

Your obligation to pay doesn't end when an unpaid debt falls off your credit report after seven years. The creditor might not be allowed to report the account, but collection actions can continue.

Similarly, your state's statute of limitations defines how long a creditor or collection agency can take you to court over a debt. But even if you can't be sued, a creditor or collector can still ask you to pay.

Given all that, shouldn't you just pay what you owe if you possibly can?

Many people would say yes, pointing out that we have a moral obligation to pay the debts we incur. But the answer to this question is actually trickier than it might appear, for several reasons.

Paying Old Debts Can Actually Hurt Your Credit Score

This seems unfair, because you're trying to make good, but that's the way credit scoring often works. When the creditor or collection agency updates your credit report to reflect the payment, the date of the new activity can make the old, troubled account look more recent to the credit scoring formula. Because the formula is designed to weigh recent behavior—good and bad— more heavily than past behavior, anything that looks like you've incurred recent problems is likely to hurt.

That really bugs Bob Brown, a mortgage broker who contacted me after seeing this phenomenon happen to his clients:

> *"It would seem that the score should improve if someone fulfills his end of the bargain by paying off a bona-fide debt," Brown said.*

Many folks would agree. Unfortunately, that's not how the formula works.

Just Contacting an Old Creditor Can Leave You Vulnerable to a Lawsuit

Each state has different guidelines on how long a creditor can sue you over a debt, but many states have provisions that allow this statute of limitations to be extended if you make a payment on an old debt or even acknowledge that you owe it. You could be making a good-faith effort to pay your bill, and the creditor could use that as an excuse to haul you into court and get a judgment against you—an action that might not have been permitted if you had just left the debt unacknowledged and unpaid. The judgment would be a new and serious black mark on your file that could be reported for another seven years.

You're Often Not Dealing with the Original Creditor

The company that you owe the money to might have long since cleared the debt off its books, taken a tax write-off for the loss, and sold the debt—usually for pennies on the dollar—to a collection agency. The original creditor might not accept money if you tried to offer it, but would instead direct you to the collector. Many people understandably feel less obligated to a collection agency that bought their debts for a tiny fraction of face value than they do to the company that originally extended the credit.

You Might Be Exposing Yourself to Some Pretty Nasty Characters

Despite laws designed to curb them, many collection agencies employ people who lie to, harass, and abuse borrowers. They might scream at you, use obscene language, or threaten you with jail time. (All of these actions are, of course, illegal, but if you don't believe they happen, you need to take a look at my mailbag.)

Even if collectors are polite to your face, they might do things behind your back to further endanger your financial life. Collectors might promise to drop a harmful remark from your credit file, and then not follow through— or make the black mark even worse. They might arrange a deal that they say will settle your debt, and then sell the unpaid portion to another agency that renews collection activity. Or they might report any debt you didn't pay to the IRS, which can tax the so-called "forgiven" debt as income.

More than a few collectors feel that anything they do is justified because—don't you know?—debtors are *bad people*. Collectors have written me insisting that debtors are actually thieves and deserve what they get. The fact that owing money is usually not illegal—but that violating fair credit reporting and collecting laws *is*—remains a distinction that completely escapes them.

You might still decide to brave all this and try to pay off an old debt. You might feel a strong moral obligation to do so, regardless of the potential consequences. Or you might need to settle a debt because you want to get a mortgage sometime soon. (Lenders typically won't give you a home loan with an open collection on your report. If you want a mortgage before the account is scheduled to drop off your report, you're probably better off paying the collection sooner rather than later, so that your score has more time to recover.)

If you decide to proceed, make sure you've done your research on the statutes of limitations that apply. (It's tricky, but you can conduct an entire settlement negotiation with a collector without ever acknowledging that you owe the debt—and most attorneys would recommend that's exactly what you should try to do.)

If you're still dealing with the original creditor, you should try to get them to report your account as positively as possible in exchange for your payment. Having the account reported "paid as agreed" would be good. Having the account reported as "settled," however, could leave your score worse off than if you'd left the account open and unpaid. Some credit repair veterans have had luck getting the creditor to stop reporting the troubled account altogether in exchange for payment, which could be great for your score, although the bureaus strongly discourage this.

If you're dealing with a collection agency, though, push hard to have the entire account deleted. You will have the most leverage if you can make a lump sum payment, rather than having to make payments. Remember: Any updating that the collection agency does—even if it's to report that you've paid your debt—can make the black mark appear more recent than it is and hurt your score.

If, on the other hand, you decide that the cost of paying old bills is greater than the payoff—well, you wouldn't be the first. Some people just decide to donate to their favorite charity an amount equal to the unpaid debt and call it a day.

"But You've Got the Wrong Guy!"

It's not uncommon for debts that you don't owe to pop up on your credit report. Thanks to identity theft, credit bureau mistakes, and greedy collection firms, this happens way too often for comfort.

But you might find yourself truly on the hook for a debt you didn't personally incur.

How can that happen? Here are two of the most common ways:

- **You cosigned a loan for someone else**—If that person doesn't pay, you're legally obligated to foot the bill, and any delinquencies, charge-offs, or collection actions that are related to the debt will be reported on your credit file. The creditor isn't even required to notify you if the other borrower defaults. The first time you find out about it might well be when it pops up on your credit report.

- **It's a joint account, even if you have since divorced the other account holder**—This one gets people all the time. It doesn't matter what your divorce decree says about who was supposed to pay what. If it's a joint account, it's a joint debt. Your ex can easily trash your report by not paying a joint credit card or mortgage. That's why it's so important to close joint accounts and refinance mortgages and other loans before a divorce is final. I'll go into more detail in Chapter 10, "Keeping Your Score Healthy."

What if you're just an authorized—rather than a joint—user on someone else's account, and that person's negative information is showing up on your report? If the person added you to the account after opening it and didn't use your income and credit information to get the credit, you should be able to get the information removed from your report.

If, however, the person used your information and forged your signature to qualify, you might need to file a police report to get the creditors to eliminate the information. See Chapter 7, "Identity Theft and Your Credit," for more details.

Part II: Adding Positive Information to Your File

There's more to credit repair than just getting rid of the negative information. You need to ensure that any positive information that can be included in your file actually is.

Try to Get Positive Accounts Reported

You know that the credit bureaus typically don't share information, but it can be frustrating if one of your good, paid-on-time accounts doesn't show up on all of your credit reports.

What's worse is when a credit account isn't reported at all. Some creditors simply don't bother to use credit bureau services, and others—usually subprime lenders—deliberately hide the histories of their best customers for fear that their competitors will swoop in.

Although you can't force a creditor to report an account to a bureau or report more frequently, you can always ask.

Sometimes it's all but impossible to get your on-time payments recorded. Most landlords, utility companies, and phone companies will only report you to the credit bureaus if you screw up. (So be sure you don't screw up.)

Borrow Someone Else's History

No, I'm not suggesting that you commit identity theft. Being added to someone else's credit card account as an authorized user can instantly improve your credit report if that person's credit is in good shape. (The opposite can also happen, so make sure you pick the right person.) A cooperative credit issuer imports the card user's account history into your report so that you can benefit from the other person's good financial habits. Not all credit issuers do this import, though, so it's important to call first and ask.

There's another plus to being an authorized, rather than a joint, user: You're not liable for any debt the original account holder runs up.

Get Some Credit or Charge Cards If You Don't Have Any

You need to actively use some plastic to rebuild your score. Although it's anybody's guess how many cards are optimal, it's a safe bet that you'll eventually need more than one—but less than a dozen.

If you still have accounts you can use, that's great. If your accounts have been closed, you'll need to start from scratch. The plan is outlined in the following sections.

Apply for a Secured Card

Secured cards give you a credit limit that's generally equal to the deposit that you make. You want a card that reports to all three credit bureaus, that doesn't charge an application fee or outrageous annual fees, and that converts to a regular, unsecured card after 12 months or so of on-time payments. Bankrate.com has a whole section on secured cards, including current information about which bank is offering what.

Get Department Store and Gas Cards

These cards tend to be the easiest unsecured plastic you can obtain. After you've had your secured card for a few months, apply for one of these—and perhaps a second one about six months later. Don't rush this process, because applying for too much credit in too short a time period can hurt your score.

Get an Installment Loan

You might take out a small, personal loan from your bank or credit bureau and pay it back over time. Or you might, as our friend Chance did, simply "suck it up" and go for a high-rate auto loan.

> *"My first vehicle loan out of BK was at 21 percent interest. After paying this for about 2 years, I traded it in and purchased another," Chance wrote. "The next [loan rate was] at 13.99 percent. [I paid] this for a year [and] then refinanced online for 7.95 percent. Then [I] traded it in, and now I have a 6 percent auto loan."*

I can't advise buying three cars in five years like Chance did. But you should try to make sure you're not tying yourself to a long-term loan at usurious rates. Get a shorter loan, if you possibly can, and make a decent down payment to make sure you have some equity in the vehicle so that you can refinance it when your credit improves.

Consider a Cosigner

If you can't get a loan on your own, you can try to find a cosigner to facilitate the deal. But realize that person is putting his credit history on the line for you. If you mess up, your cosigner pays the price, because they're just as legally obligated to pay the debt as you are.

Make Sure Your Credit Limits Are Correct

This is a point that many credit rebuilders unfortunately overlook. A big chunk of your credit score has to do with how much of your available credit you're using. If the credit limits are showing up on your report as lower than they actually are, your debt utilitization ratio will be higher than it needs to be. You can use the dispute process, but it might be just as expeditious to call your creditors and ask them to update your credit bureau files.

Part III: Use Your Credit Well

You might want to review the information in Chapter 3 on improving your score the right way. When you're rebuilding after a disaster, you need to be particularly careful about what's discussed in this section.

Pay Bills on Time

Remember: The biggest chunk of your credit score is likely to be your payment history, and even one late payment can be devastating. Become religious about making sure all your bills are paid on time, all the time.

If you get an installment loan, set up an automatic payment system—either direct withdrawals from your checking account or automatic, recurring payments through an online bill paying system. Leave nothing to chance.

Use the Credit You Have

Make a few small purchases every month with your plastic—but no more than you can pay off each month. If you worry that you'll give in to temptation if you carry your card with you, arrange to have some small monthly bill, such as your newspaper subscription or health club dues, charged to the card each month. Then set up an automatic payment from your checking account. That way the card is being used and the bill is being paid without your having to think about it.

Keep Your Balances Low

Somebody who has good credit can occasionally afford to run up a big balance on a credit card. You, my dear, cannot. It doesn't matter if your credit limits on your new cards are ridiculously low. You never want to use more than about 30 percent of the limits you have.

How will you know? You can keep track of your purchases in a checkbook register, or just check your balances frequently at the card's Web site. Personal finance software such as Quicken or Money can also help you keep track.

Remember: These cards are not for your convenience—and they certainly shouldn't be an excuse for you to carry debt. The plastic you have now is meant to help rehabilitate your beaten-up credit.

Pace Yourself

It's never a good idea to apply for a bunch of new credit in a short period of time. That's particularly true when you're trying to rebuild a score. It's not a bad idea to wait at least six months between applications for credit. Don't apply for cards just to see if you'll be accepted, and do try to target your applications to lenders that are likely to want your business. A recently bankrupted person who applies for a low-rate card from a major issuer is just asking to get turned down—and have another ding added to his or her file.

Don't Commit the Biggest Credit Repair Mistakes

You can see from the information in this chapter that fixing your credit can be a long and involved process, with many opportunities for the novice to make a mistake. Three of the biggest mistakes you should avoid are spelled out below.

Hiring a Fly-by-Night Firm

The Federal Trade Commission is constantly trying to stamp out scam artists promising instant credit repair, but like cockroaches, they always return. You can pretty much assume a scam if the company guarantees its results in advance, wants to charge you a big, upfront fee, or suggests you create a "new" credit report by using a different Social Security or taxpayer identification number.

Most people can handle their own credit repair without paying big fees or committing fraud. If you run into problems, look for a legitimate law firm through the National Association of Consumer Advocates at www.naca.net for help.

Failing to Get It All in Writing

The phone is not your friend. Although you can and should take copious notes if you ever have to have a phone conversation with a creditor, collector, or credit bureau, you're much better off conducting credit repair in writing.

Reviving the Statute of Limitations

States have differing rules about how long a creditor can sue you over a debt, with most limiting the period to three to six years. Making a payment on an old debt, or even acknowledging that you owe it, can revive that statute and leave you vulnerable to a lawsuit. Make sure you know the rules for your state when dealing with old debts.

7

IDENTIFY THEFT AND YOUR CREDIT

Identity theft is such a rapidly-growing crime that some experts say it's no longer a matter of *whether* you'll become a victim—it's a matter of *when*.

The Federal Trade Commission, which once estimated that identity theft affected 700,000 to 1 million Americans each year, announced in 2003 that the problem was vastly greater than it had guessed. In fact, an FTC-commissioned survey found that 27.3 million Americans have been victimized in the past five years, including 9.9 million people in the past year alone.

The annual costs of this crime are staggering:

- $48 billion in annual losses for business and institutions

- $5 billion in out-of-pocket expenses for consumers

- 300 million hours spent by consumers trying to resolve the problem, stop the fraud, and clear up their credit reports

Identity theft encompasses a variety of crimes, from stealing someone's credit card number to opening accounts in the victim's name. About 15 percent of victims report that their identities were stolen for purposes other than obtaining credit, such as to get government documents, commit tax fraud, or mislead police. It's relatively common, for example, for someone to give a phony name and Social Security number when arrested or stopped for a traffic violation.

Thieves tend to do the most damage when they can take over your identity wholesale. By pretending to be you, they can open up credit card accounts, get an auto loan, be treated at a hospital, or rent an apartment. When the bills are due, they don't pay—and those delinquencies, charge-offs, collections, repossessions, evictions, and judgments wind up on your credit report, sending your credit score into the basement.

This kind of "new account" theft costs, on average, $10,200 per victim and makes up nearly 70 percent of the costs incurred by businesses and financial institutions. The out-of-pocket expenses for consumers tend to be higher as well—$1,200 compared to the average $500 when all types of identity theft are considered.

The FTC's estimate of the time that consumers spend clearing up problems—30 hours on average—was decried by many identity theft experts as far too low. The Identity Theft Resource Center said that many victims spend 300 to 600 hours dealing with the various problems that identity thieves cause.

Often, the biggest time-consumer is trying to get fraudulent accounts expunged from credit reports. Many victims complain they get the runaround from credit bureaus. The bureaus say the problem is lenders, who continue to report account information to the bureaus even after they've been told the accounts might be fraudulent. Either way, the ID theft victim gets squeezed. Michel, a successful businessman in Sherman Oaks, California, spent months trying to convince the three credit bureaus to remove delinquent accounts from his credit report before finally hiring a lawyer.

"It took me almost a year and thousands of dollars to finally clean up my report. In the meantime, I lost out on the lowest mortgage rates in years as a result," Michel said. "The whole system is totally unfair as the three majors believe the creditors and make it virtually impossible to remove an item unless you hire an attorney."

Michel might overstate the case, but he does reflect the frustration experienced by many identity theft victims trying to clear their names, said Linda Foley, codirector of the Identity Theft Resource Center and an ID theft victim herself.

Even if you're successful in getting your reports cleaned up, your work might not be done. After identity thieves find someone who has good credit, they can strike over and over again. Mary in Charlotte, North Carolina, has been hit four times so far.

"I do everything the experts say," Mary said. "I have a shredder . . . I don't even mail bills from my home."

Although three of the incidents involved existing accounts, the fourth involved new credit cards.

"The criminal racked up thousands in credit card debt under my name . . . and had the bills mailed somewhere else," Mary said.

Mary was clueless about the debt until she tried to apply for a cell phone and was turned down.

Here are just a few of the ways your identity can be stolen:

- You hand your credit card to a waiter in a restaurant. Out of your sight, the waiter runs the card through a small, handheld device called a skimmer. All of the relevant information contained on your card's black magnetic strip—including your name and the account number—is stored in the device and can be used to create new cards.

- You fill out an application for credit, an apartment, insurance, or employment. A crooked employee sells the information to a ring of identity thieves or uses it herself to open accounts. Or perhaps the employees are honest, but the business tosses the application into the trash, where any dumpster diver could find it.

- Hackers break into online databases where your personal financial data is stored. In February 2003, one such thief accessed eight million credit card numbers stored by a company that processes transactions for Visa, MasterCard, American Express, and Discover. Another hacker snuck into a California state government database and scored the names and Social Security numbers of 265,000 state employees, including the governor and all 120 legislators.

- Thieves pretending to be legitimate lenders—or again, dishonest employees of actual lenders—obtain credit reports from the bureaus and use the information to open new accounts. One example: Thieves posing as Ford Motor Credit Co. personnel stole credit reports for more than 30,000 consumers, causing at least $2.7 million in losses.

You might notice a common thread to these examples: There's precious little you, as an individual, could have done to prevent these crimes.

Sure, you could stop using plastic at restaurants, refuse to fill out any more applications, and cancel all of your credit cards, but there's still enough information about you floating around out there for a thief to use.

This is a point missed in most identity theft articles, which tend to focus on simplistic solutions like "Buy a shredder!" and "Get a locking mailbox!" Yes, these measures can help, and later in the chapter you'll find quite a few more preventative suggestions. But they don't change the fact that much of your exposure to identity theft is beyond your control.

If you really want to see why identity theft is epidemic, look no further than your own wallet. Chances are if you have one credit card, you have five, and just about every chain store you walk into is trying to get you to apply for another. Lenders are so desperate to extend credit that they offer instant credit, send out billions of preapproved applications, and mail customers so-called "convenience checks" that thieves can fish out of the mail or trash. You've probably heard the stories about dogs being sent credit card applications; Diane of Santa Barbara recently got one for her two-year-old.

"I could not and still cannot believe that credit card companies are not held more responsible for giving out credit," Diane said, "without truly checking the background of the individuals to whom they provide credit."

Even without a prefilled form, identity thieves have discovered that getting approved for new credit is pretty easy. Many lenders don't require photo IDs, and some accept incorrect addresses and misspelled names. Often all the thief needs is your Social Security number and an approximate spelling of your name.

Tom Richards of Huntington Beach, California, said a thief convinced Sears by phone to issue two MasterCards in Richards' name—and then send them to an address not listed on Richards' credit report.

The application was fishy enough that Sears sent a letter to Richards' actual address, informing him that the cards had been issued. That allowed Richards to report the fraud. But it made him wonder why Sears would open the account in the first place.

Simply put, the answer is money. The more credit that lenders and retailers can extend, the more money they can make. Speed is key, and most lenders' computerized processes are designed to make decisions in minutes, if not seconds. If the decisions are wrong, most lenders can easily absorb the costs of the resulting fraud. The costs that consumers pay—in out-of-pocket expenses, time, and legal fees trying to clear up their credit reports—aren't taken into account.

Incredibly enough, some lenders are in such a hurry that they even ignore fraud alerts, which are the flags that identity theft victims can put on their credit reports to let lenders know their credit has been misused and to indicate that they want to be contacted personally if credit applications are submitted in their names. Some lenders feel the extra step is too expensive, whereas others never see the alert, because they buy truncated credit information that doesn't include the red flag.

All these problems finally prompted Congress to pass new laws in 2003 that might help identity theft victims get back some control of their lives. Most of these changes, contained in the Fair and Accurate Credit Transactions Act (FACTA), will be phased in over time, so it's too early to tell how effective they'll be. According to a summation by Consumers Union, the law includes the following provisions:

- If a fraud alert is on a consumer's credit report, lenders will be required to phone the consumer or take other "reasonable steps" to verify the applicant's identity before issuing credit or raising a credit limit. The alert must be included with any credit report or score sold to lenders.

- Any consumer will be able to put a 90-day fraud alert on his or her credit file. The alert can be extended for 7 years if the consumer provides an *identity theft report*, such as the ID theft affidavit provided by the Federal Trade Commission, as long as the report is filed with a local police agency. Those who file for extended alerts are automatically kept off the marketing lists that bureaus sell to credit card companies and other lenders.

- When a consumer files a fraud alert with one bureau, that bureau will be required to contact the others so that alerts can be put on their records as well.

- Credit bureaus will be required to stop reporting accounts or account information that a consumer identifies as fraudulent if the consumer provides an identity theft report filed with a police agency. This procedure is known as *trade line blocking*.

- After a bureau informs a creditor that a block is in effect, the creditor must have "reasonable" procedures to keep it from reporting the bad information again and "repolluting" the consumer's file.

- When a block is in effect, creditors will not be able to sell or transfer the debt to a collection agency. If the debt is already in collections, the collector will be required to notify the original creditor that the debt might be fraudulent and to provide the consumer a notice of his or her collection rights— if the consumer asks for such a notice.

- Businesses where a thief has opened accounts will have new
  duties to produce records that the ID theft victim might need
  to clear his name. The businesses, however, might require the
  ID theft victim to get an actual police report (which is different,
  and more difficult to get, than an affidavit filed with a
  police agency).

- Credit card machines will be required to truncate all credit
  and debit card numbers on receipts by 2007, and consumers
  will be able to request that the credit reports sent to them
  truncate Social Security numbers.

Will these measures help? Identity theft experts worry that Congress
gave lenders several big loopholes, such as allowing them to take "reasonable
steps" for identity verification rather than requiring phone contact. They note
that many law enforcement agencies still refuse to take identity theft seriously
and won't create police reports or accept affidavits. They point out that creditors
and credit bureaus are already prohibited from reporting false information by
the Fair Credit Reporting Act. If those laws haven't worked, they wonder,
how will the new laws?

Time will tell. In the meantime, you need to be vigilant about monitoring and protecting your credit.

How to Reduce Your Exposure to Identity Theft

There are several things that you can do to reduce the possibility of having
your identity stolen.

Buy a Shredder

You can get a shredder for less than $20 at an office supply store, and no
home should be without one. Any piece of paper that includes personal financial information or your Social Security number should be shredded before
it's sent to the trash.

Get a Locking Mailbox

Think of all the bounty that comes into your mailbox—bank statements, credit cards, credit card offers, "convenience checks" you can write against your accounts, health insurance documents with your Social Security numbers printed on them . . . the list goes on and on. Many identity thieves simply follow the postal carrier around and snatch what they want from unprotected mailboxes.

Protect Your Outgoing Mail

Think of all that goes out in your mail, including checks and credit card account numbers on the coupons you use to pay your bills. If you still rely on snail mail to pay your bills, use the post office nearest to you to send all your mail, rather than leaving it out where anyone can get it. Better yet, consider signing up for online bill payment, which offers encryption and other security measures to keep your transactions safe from criminals. (Hacking incidents typically target big unencrypted databases sitting in poorly guarded mainframe computers, not the heavily protected transactions that zip back and forth between consumers and their banks or merchants.)

Keep Track of Your Receipts

All that a dumpster diver needs to find is a credit card receipt with your full account number printed on it, and he's struck gold. These so-called "flimsies" have pretty good street value when sold to identity thieves.

As mentioned before, federal FACTA legislation won't require merchants to truncate credit card numbers on receipts until 2007. Even then, some won't change their systems. I still occasionally get receipts with my full credit card number printed on them, even though a similar law has been in effect in my state of California for a few years now.

Keep Your Financial Documents Under Lock and Key

How easy would it be for a repairman to walk off with your checkbook, or for a guest in your home to rifle through your files? Most people are perfectly trustworthy, but enough aren't that you should take steps to secure your checks and files.

Get Stingy with Your Social Security Number

This nine-digit number was never meant to be an all-purpose identifier, but that's exactly how many businesses use it. Everyone from your dry cleaner to your vet might ask for it, but few have the right to demand it.

You need to give your Social Security number to employers, financial institutions, and certain government agencies, such as your state's Department of Motor Vehicles. Your Social Security number is also important for credit transactions. Many insurers use the number as an identifier, or to run credit checks to determine your premiums (see Chapter 9, "Insurance and Your Credit Score").

Beyond that, though, you should try to keep your number to yourself. If the business insists that it needs the number, you can either do business with someone else or "misremember" a digit or nine to protect your privacy.

Know What's in Your Wallet

Obviously, you shouldn't carry your Social Security number with you or have it printed on your checks. You should also lobby your health insurer to print "Participant's SSN" instead of the actual number on your card. This system is working fine in California, which is leading the nation in privacy protections by insisting that health insurers stop printing the numbers on health cards by 2005. Many have done so well before the deadline.

Beyond that, you should try to carry as few credit and debit cards as possible. The more you carry, the more chances that an identity thief has to wreck your credit if your wallet is stolen.

If you have your wallet stolen, don't wait until you get home to report stolen credit cards. Grab your cell or the nearest phone and call 1-800-VISA 911 to report missing Visa cards and 1-800-MasterCard to report stolen MasterCards. These are among the most valuable cards to thieves and should be shut down right away. When you get home (or back to your hotel, if you're traveling), you can work on canceling the rest.

It can help to periodically empty your wallet onto a photocopier and get an image of both sides of every card, plus your driver's license. This will make it easier for you to report the thefts and get replacement cards. (Just remember to put the cards back in your wallet and keep copies in a safe place. You don't want to leave your financial life laying around at the local Kinko's.)

Ask About Shredding Policies

If you're required to give personal financial information to any business or professional, ask how they dispose of old documents. If the business doesn't have a shredding policy in place, take your business elsewhere or press it to institute one. In Georgia and California, state laws don't allow businesses to discard records with personal information unless they first shred or erase the records, or modify them to make the data unreadable. Wisconsin has a similar law that applies to financial institutions, tax preparers, and companies with medical information.

It's not too much to ask, for example, that your accountant shred copies of your old tax returns, or at least call you so that you can come pick them up and do the same. Ditto for your doctor or any other professional.

Don't Let Your Debit Card Out of Your Sight

If your ATM card has a Visa or MasterCard logo, it's known as a debit or check card and can be used just like a credit card, without punching in a personal identification number. A thief who swipes it or skims the information off the magnetic stripe can quickly empty your bank account.

The good news is that banks won't hold you responsible for fraud committed with a debit card with a Visa or MasterCard logo, but you can still wind up without money for a few days before the bank restores the stolen cash. That's why it's better to use a credit card or cash anywhere you won't be able to monitor the actual transaction (such as when you hand payment to a waiter in a restaurant).

Mary, the four-time identity theft victim, also refuses to use her debit card at fast food restaurants, gas stations, or mom-and-pop type stores.

"These small business do not do background checks on employees, they typically have high turnover rates, and [they] are prime targets for transient-type workers," Mary said. "Any criminal [who] engages in identity theft for a living knows they can wait tables for a month and get tons of card numbers to use or sell."

This should be obvious, but don't give your credit or debit cards to anyone else to use. A small but significant portion of fraud and identity theft is committed by family members, friends, and lovers—either current or ex. Some of the most heartbreaking cases are when a parent snatches the identity of a child (see "When Parents Steal," later in this chapter).

Opt Out of Credit Card Solicitations, Junk Mail, and Telemarketing

The credit bureaus have a toll-free number (888-5OPT-OUT) that allows you to take your name off marketing lists that are sold to credit card companies. Signing up won't eliminate credit card solicitations, but it will cut down the volume significantly. The fewer such offers in the mail, the fewer chances that thieves will have to steal them.

You can contact the Direct Marketing Association to be removed from their mail and phone lists, as well. Write to Mail Preference Service, P.O. Box 643, Carmel, NY 10512 and Telephone Preference Service, P.O. Box 1559, Carmel, NY 10512. Even better, to all but eliminate telephone solicitations, register for the federal do-not-call list at www.donotcall.gov or 1-888- 382-1222. If a solicitor calls you after you've been on the registry at least three months—and the caller isn't a charity, survey-taker, political fundraiser, or a company that you already do business with—odds are good it's a scam artist, because a legitimate company would abide by the do-not-call list.

Don't Use a Cell or Cordless Phone to Discuss Financial Matters

It's pretty easy to intercept wireless signals—or simply to overhear any conversation when you're booming along at your local coffeehouse.

Be Wary of Telephone Solicitors and Emails Purporting to Be from Financial Institutions

Don't give out your credit card number, Social Security number, or other sensitive financial information by email, and don't do it by phone unless you initiated the contact. Even then, make sure that you trust the business before divulging any information.

Criminals have become increasingly proficient at *phishing*, a fraud that typically uses an email purporting to be from your bank or credit card issuer and that directs you to a look-alike Web site where you're supposed to input your account numbers. If a financial institution contacts you, call them using the toll-free number on your statement rather than a number provided on an email or Web site.

Monitor Your Social Security Statements

Each year, a few months before your birthday, you should receive a statement from the Social Security Administration summarizing your earnings during your working years, plus an estimate of the benefits you and your family can expect. The statements are sent automatically to workers and former workers 25 and older. If you meet those criteria and aren't getting statements, you should call the SSA immediately at 1-800-772-1213 to request the latest copy and make sure your contact information is correct.

It is a good idea to review your statement to make sure you're being properly credited for all the taxes you've paid into the system, but it can also help you spot fraud. Missing earnings or earnings that aren't yours can be a tip-off.

Don't worry too much, though, if your previous year's earnings seem too low. It sometimes takes a while for the SSA to update its information. If that year's earnings are still too low when you get your next statement, contact the SSA.

Monitor Your Credit Reports

A few years ago, it was enough to check your credit report annually. Now, many identity theft experts recommend that you review your reports at least twice a year, if not more often. The first hint you might have that you're a victim is often a suspicious entry on your credit report.

Should you spring for one of those credit-monitoring services that promise to do the work for you? Maybe not. Read on.

Does Credit Monitoring Work?

The public's rising concern about identity theft has prompted the credit bureaus and other companies to see a lucrative marketing opportunity. The result is credit monitoring, or services that promise to watch over your credit report and alert you if anything suspicious occurs.

Almost nonexistent 10 years ago, credit monitoring and similar "privacy-protection" services are now a $2.5-billion industry, according to the Center for Social & Legal Research, a nonpartisan research organization.

What credit monitoring can't do is *prevent* identity theft, despite marketers' claims that it provides "protection" against such crimes. Credit monitoring services can't snatch credit applications out of thieves' hands or prevent lenders from opening accounts for the wrong people. What the better services can do is give you some early warning that there's a problem, which can give you a head start in cleaning up the mess.

The quality, however, varies widely, and most credit monitoring services have serious drawbacks:

- **They're not comprehensive**—The better services promise to check your report at all three credit bureaus, but typically they provide ongoing monitoring of your report at only one bureau, with only periodic checks of the other two. These periodic checks usually happen once every three months, but they might be annual. Some services stick solely to one bureau and never check in at the other two.

- **They might not provide much of a head start**—The best services promise to alert you within 24 hours if someone applies for credit in your name. Others settle for weekly, monthly, or even quarterly updates. Again, because most don't provide daily monitoring of all three bureaus, ID theft might not be detected for months.

- **They're costly**—At this writing, the cheapest services cost more than $40 a year for a single bureau's credit report that's updated quarterly. The more comprehensive services cost more than $100 a year for daily monitoring of one bureau's report, and quarterly updates of the others. To get ongoing monitoring of all three bureaus, you'd need to subscribe to several different services and pay more than $200 a year.

It's possible that credit monitoring services will get cheaper and more comprehensive as consumers catch on to these flaws. Also, the new FACTA legislation mandates that everyone be allowed a free credit report annually from each of the three bureaus—a reality that might cut into the credit monitoring business and force it to improve. (Of course, the FACTA legislation also allows credit bureaus to pitch monitoring services and other products to anyone who requests free reports, so the services might not feel a great need to innovate.)

Many ID theft experts suggest that most people are better off requesting their reports periodically from the bureaus, rather than paying for credit monitoring. Credit expert Jay Foley of the Identity Theft Resource Center suggests rotating your requests, so that you first get a report from Experian, then three months later one from TransUnion, and then three months after that one from Equifax. If you keep up the rotation, you'll see each bureau's report at least twice every 12 months for much less than you'd pay a credit-monitoring service.

If you do decide you want a monitoring service's help, though, make sure you find out the following:

* How often your report is checked at each bureau, and how often those reports are updated.

* How quickly you'll be sent an email if something suspicious occurs. Find out the longest that a problem could appear on your report at any of the bureaus before the service would bring it to your attention.

* How much the service costs and how often you will be charged.

* What other services are provided (identity theft insurance, concierge help in reporting identity theft) and how you can access those services.

What to Do If You're Already a Victim

The only good news about the rise in identity theft is that there are now more resources than ever before to help victims. You still need to gird yourself for battle with credit bureaus, creditors, and even collection agencies, but you're not out there alone.

The Federal Trade Commission has extensive information for ID theft victims at www.consumer.gov/idtheft, or you can call 1-877-FTC-HELP (1-877-382-4357) to get free information. You also can find helpful resources at the Identity Theft Resource Center (www.idtheftcenter.org or 1-858-693-7935) and the Privacy Rights Clearinghouse (www.privacyrights.org or 1-619-298-3396), among other locations.

Some financial institutions are remarkably responsive to identity theft victims, whereas others presume that anyone reporting ID theft is a liar until proven otherwise. Either way, you'll want to be assertive, persistent, and relentless in your efforts to clear your name. The Privacy Rights Clearing-house, the California Public Interest Research Group, and the Identity Theft Resource Center suggest that you take the steps outlined in the next sections.

Keep Good Notes of Every Conversation You Have Regarding the ID Theft

Include dates, times, and first and last names, if possible, of everyone you contact. (It can be helpful to use one notebook in which you jot everything down, so your notes aren't scattered all over the house.) Follow up these conversations in writing, with letters sent certified mail, return receipt requested. Keep track of the hours and costs you're incurring; you might be eligible for restitution if the thief is caught and prosecuted.

Contact the Credit Bureaus By Phone and Then with a Follow-Up in Writing

In most cases, you'll want to add a fraud alert to your credit file and to make sure the alert is for 7 years, rather than any shorter period. Fraud alerts can make "instant" credit more difficult to obtain, but you can always cancel an alert later if you want.

The bureaus now have a system whereby you need to contact only one for the other two to be notified. Take your choice: You can call Equifax at 800-525-6285, Experian at 888-397-3742, or TransUnion at 800-680-7289. The credit bureaus are required to send you a free credit report when you add a fraud alert.

The credit bureaus should be able to supply you with contact information for any creditors that are listed on your credit report.

At this writing, you also have the option, if you're a California resident, of putting a "freeze" on your credit reports. This freeze prevents anyone from accessing your credit report for any reason. You will be issued a personal identification number to "unlock" your file when you need to apply for credit. The freeze is free for ID theft victims and available for a fee to anyone else. The California Office of Privacy Protection at www.privacy.ca.gov has more information.

Contact the Creditors By Phone and Then with a Follow-Up in Writing

If someone is using one of your existing credit or bank accounts to run up charges, the bank or lender typically closes the account and issues you a new one, along with some kind of form or affidavit to report the fraud. If new accounts have been opened, the financial institution also asks you to fill out a fraud affidavit. Many accept the uniform fraud affidavit available on the FTC Web site.

Contact the Police or Local Sheriff

Some jurisdictions are terrific about taking identity theft reports, and some aren't—even though it's a federal crime (18 USC 1028) to assume someone else's identity. Be persistent, bring as much documentation of the fraud as you can, and try to get the law enforcement agency to list the affected accounts on the report. A police report can help enormously in getting problems resolved with creditors.

Contact Bank and Checking Verification Companies

If the thief set up phony bank accounts in your name or stole checks, you need to close those accounts and stop payment on any outstanding checks. Open new checking and savings accounts and contact the major check verification companies to report the theft. Here are some of those companies:

- **CheckRite**—800-766-2748

- **ChexSystems**—800-428-9623

- **Certigy**—800-437-5120

- **International Check Services**—800-526-5380

- **TeleCheck**—800-710-9898

Contact the Collection Agencies

FACTA legislation will make it illegal for fraudulent accounts to be turned over to collections, but that doesn't mean it won't happen—or doesn't help you much if it's happened already.

Dealing with collection agencies can be especially difficult, because they're used to dealing with bad debts every day, and have heard every excuse in the book—including many false claims of identity theft. In addition, more than a few collectors are unresponsive, unethical, and abusive in their dealings with consumers. Tread carefully here, but don't give up. The Identity Theft Resource Center has a separate fact sheet (FS 116) on how to cope. The following are some of the suggestions:

- In addition to keeping good notes and following up in writing (certified mail, return receipt requested), ask for a written statement from the collector outlining any agreements or decisions you discuss. Ask for confirmation in writing that you don't owe the debt and that the account has been closed.

- Stay cool and calm. The more professional you act, the more likely the collection agency will treat you seriously.

- Ask for a supervisor or the company's fraud investigator. Customer service representatives are usually little help.

- Tell the collector that you are a victim of identity theft and you are not responsible for the account. Don't say that you "dispute" the account, because collection agencies associate that word with people who are arguing about the amounts they owe or trying to evade a legitimate debt.

Collection protocols for dealing with identity theft are constantly evolving, so contact the center for more details on your rights and the best approaches.

Get Legal Help

If your efforts to solve the problem yourself aren't working, you might need to hire a lawyer. You can get referrals from your local bar, legal aid office, or the National Association of Consumer Advocates at 202-452-1989.

Don't Give Up

Be determined to be the last one standing when this is over. Don't pay bills that aren't yours to get a creditor off your back and don't file for bankruptcy. If a creditor or collector threatens you with a lawsuit, jail time, or other punishment, point out calmly that such threats are violations of federal debt collecting and credit reporting laws. Then report them to the Federal Trade Commission and your state attorney general's office.

When Parents Steal

Michelle was a Kentucky college student in 2001 when she discovered an awful fact: Her credit score had been trashed by her mother, who had taken out more than 10 credit cards in Michelle's name and failed to pay debts totaling more than $12,000.

"No one would believe me, not police, judges, lawyers," Michelle said. "I was harassed by collectors telling me I was a liar."

Michelle has since found a lawyer who's trying, for free, to help her clear her name. But it's an uphill battle. Although several of the accounts were opened when Michelle was under 18—a minor and obviously too young to be held to a contract—many of the credit card companies are refusing to drop the black marks from her credit report.

"I have spent so much time in tears, worry, depression, and rage over this ordeal," Michelle said. "I can't get a new credit card, and when I moved off campus last year, my roommate had to sign the lease because my credit was too bad to get an apartment."

What's worse, Michelle said, is her mother's reaction to the chaos she created in her daughter's life.

"To this day," Michelle said, "she still will not admit she did anything wrong."

Unfortunately, Michelle's experience is far from unique. Some parents intercept credit card applications meant for their adult children and then add themselves to the accounts. Others use their minor children's Social Security numbers to get utilities, cell phones, or new credit cards. Often, the crimes can continue for years before the victims have any clue what happened—or understand the price that they'll pay.

Like Michelle, Amy was in college when she discovered her mother had opened credit cards in Amy's name.

"At the time, I had threatened to go to the authorities, but I was talked out of it by my father," Amy said.

It wasn't until Amy finished graduate school and tried to get an apartment and a car that she began to realize the full extent of the damage.

The crimes have created a "permanent rift" in Amy's family and left her feeling betrayed, violated, and isolated.

"For years I was ashamed of this and never spoke up when family members believed . . . the stories [my mother] told of our estrangement," Amy said.

Parental thieves put their victims into a horrific bind in other ways. Many creditors won't drop a fraudulent account unless the victim files a police report, which could result in the arrest and prosecution of the parent. Few children are willing to take that step.

Katie finally did after being repeatedly victimized by her mother. The older woman first drained Katie's credit union account, and then she applied for utilities in Katie's name.

"At that time, I didn't really know what to do," Katie said. "No one I knew had ever been in that situation."

It wasn't until Katie and her husband applied for a mortgage, and two more fraudulent accounts appeared on Katie's credit report, that she finally took action.

"I got the police report, spoke to three different lawyers about what I should do, contacted each credit bureau and collection agency," Katie said. "Two of the three accounts have been taken off my record. I'm still waiting to hear about the third account."

Katie's mom hasn't been arrested, but Katie has little faith that the experience has changed the older woman.

"I really am worried that this will happen again in the future," to Katie or to someone else, Katie said. "She will find someone to latch on to and use them until they find out about it."

What to Do If the Credit Bureau Won't Budge

Kay in Valley View, Texas, lost her adult daughter seven years ago to a blood clot. Wanting to do the right thing, Kay paid off a loan she'd cosigned with her daughter.

Ever since then, however, the three credit bureaus all list Kay as "deceased." Kay's credit file has been mixed with that of her daughter's, and as a result, Kay can't get credit.

"I have no FICO score," Kay wrote. "I have tried and tried to get it changed. Several times I sent [the bureaus] copies of phone bills, electric bills, Social Security papers, driver's license, on and on, everything I've been asked to send. [It's] still not resolved."

It shouldn't be that hard to prove you're alive, or correct any other mistake in your credit file, for that matter. But sometimes, it is. If you've followed the suggestions in this book and are still slamming into a brick wall, you might need to take extraordinary measures.

Here's what can help:

- **Resolve to be the last person standing**—Many people are appalled at the amount of time and energy it can take to get the simplest problem solved. Those who are tenacious to the point of obsession are in the best position to wear the opposition down. The bureaus, creditors, and collection agencies are counting on you to go away after a few rebuffs; credit repair veterans say they often win their cases by repeatedly refusing to take "no" for an answer.

- **Consult with those who have gone before**—The best tactics for winning the battle change constantly as all sides adjust their strategies. Checking out credit repair sites like CreditBoards.com, which can give you some ideas and strategies from people who have some experience fighting the same battles. Just remember to take everything you read with a grain of salt—anyone can post on these boards.

- **Get a lawyer's help**—It's not easy to find a good attorney who's up on the nuances of the Fair Credit Reporting Act and the Fair Debt Collection Practices Act. But they're out there. Once again, you can get referrals from your local bar, legal aid office, or the National Association of Consumer Advocates at 202-452-1989.

  Even if your lawyer isn't crackerjack, the other side might take you more seriously if correspondence about your case suddenly starts coming on the letterhead of Willgetya, Butgood, & Howe.

- **Get Congress involved**—Many people are surprised to learn that their U.S. Representative is willing to weigh in on consumer issues, and most maintain a staff to help their constituents.

  Don't expect your elected representative to get excited about aiding your campaign to delete a $99 collection from your credit report. But if your story has any outrage factor at all— why can't the bureaus figure out you're alive, or not your father, or the victim of identity theft?—you might be able to enlist their help.

- **Call a local newspaper, television, or radio reporter**— Most media outlets have someone who covers finance or consumer issues. An ongoing battle with a credit bureau can be a juicy story, if told correctly. Be as succinct as you can when contacting the reporter (by email is usually best). If you don't get a response, follow up politely in a few weeks to ask if they can refer you to anyone else.

  You'll probably have the best luck at a smaller newspaper, station, or Web site. Reporters and columnists at large outlets get so many of these sad stories that they can only follow up on a fraction of the leads. Like the big regulators, they usually wait for a pattern of specific abuses to develop before they act, so your letter might or might not ever get answered. That doesn't mean you shouldn't try, but if you get no response, aim for a smaller media outlet closer to home.

8

EMERGENCY! FIXING YOUR CREDIT SCORE FAST

If you've read this far, you know what a tedious process fixing errors on your credit report can be.

Credit bureaus have 30 days to investigate complaints and often defer to what lenders say about you, whether or not it's true. Even if all parties agree that a mistake has been made, the errors can continue to crop up in your file thanks to the automated nature of most credit reporting. You might have to contact creditors and the bureaus several times to get inaccuracies deleted. The process usually takes weeks; at worst, you might be fighting the battle for months or even years.

If you're in the midst of trying to get a mortgage, these errors can cause serious problems. You might not have enough time to fix your report before the house falls out of escrow or you get stuck with an interest rate much higher than you deserve to pay.

Troubles like these might tempt you to turn to one of the many companies that promise "instant credit repair" or that guarantee to boost your credit score. No legitimate company makes such promises or guarantees, though, so anyone who hires one of these outfits is begging to be scammed.

There are, however, a growing number of genuine services that really *can* fix mistakes on your credit report in 72 hours or less. Read on to learn more.

Repairing Your Credit in a Matter of Hours: Rapid Rescoring

Rapid rescoring services came about because too many people were losing loans or paying too much interest because of credit bureau inaccuracies. Before you get excited, though, you should learn what these services can and can't do:

- **They can't deal with you directly as a consumer**—Rapid rescoring is typically offered by small credit reporting agencies, which serve as a kind of middleman between the bureaus and the lending professionals.

  These agencies, which are often independent but which might be subsidiaries of credit bureaus, provide special services for loan officers and mortgage brokers such as merged or "3-in-1" credit reports. To benefit from rapid rescoring, you need to be working with a loan officer or mortgage broker who subscribes to an agency that offers the service.

- **They can help you only if you have proof, or if proof can be obtained**—Rapid rescoring services aren't designed to help people who have yet to start the credit repair process. You need something in writing, such as a letter from the creditor acknowledging that your account was reported as late when you were in fact on time. (This is one of the reasons that it's so important to get everything in writing when you're trying to fix your credit.) If you don't have such proof, but the creditor has acknowledged the error, some rapid rescorers can get the proof for you. However, that might add days or weeks to the process.

- **They can help you get errors fixed, but they can't remove true negative items that are in dispute**—Again, you need proof that a mistake was made—not just your say-so. If the credit bureau is already investigating your complaint about an error, the item typically can't be included in a rapid rescoring process.

- **They can't promise to help your score**—As you read in Chapter 2, "How Credit Scoring Works," sometimes removing negative items can actually hurt a score—strange as that might seem.

The scoring formula tries to compare you to people who have similar credit histories. If you've been lumped into the group with a bankruptcy or other black marks on your report, you might find that your score *falls* when some of those negative items are removed. Instead of being at the top of the bankrupts' group, in other words, you've dropped to the bottom of the next group—the folks who have better credit.

More commonly, removing an error might not help your score as much as you might have hoped and might not win you a better interest rate. There are no guarantees with rapid rescoring.

But Doug in Phoenix is one of the many borrowers who have benefited so far. Doug filed for bankruptcy in 1998, but several of his wiped-out debts were still shown as open and unpaid on his credit report five years later when he applied for a mortgage.

Technically, the accounts all should have been reported as "included in bankruptcy." It's a common enough error, and one that can usually be fixed— if you have a month or more.

Doug didn't. He worried that he would lose the house he wanted to buy and perhaps miss out on some of the lowest rates borrowers had seen in years. Doug's mortgage broker used his bankruptcy papers to prove the errors to a rapid rescoring service, which fixed the problems and boosted Doug's score.

The rate he got—just over 7 percent—was still higher than someone who had good credit would have received at the time, but it was much better than the rate he might have received without the fix.

This is exactly the kind of intervention that the National Association of Mortgage Brokers was hoping for when it began agitating in 1997 for a way to speed up the dispute process and keep old, proven errors from killing mortgage deals. Congress had made some updates to the Fair Credit Reporting Act in 1996 that were supposed to help consumers, but the problems remained widespread.

Once upon a time, brokers and other lending professionals could do something about these problems. In the days before the widespread use of a credit score, a broker or loan officer could intervene to convince a lender to ignore mistakes or small blemishes on a client's credit file. Everyone involved understood that credit report errors were common, and having an experienced loan pro vouch for your credit-worthiness could often get a deal done.

With the advent of credit scoring and automated loan processes, though, those opportunities to advocate for clients quickly evaporated. Lending professionals shared consumers' frustration when erroneous information continued to be reported by the bureaus—information that often dampened credit scores and resulted in worse rates and terms than the borrower deserved.

The mortgage brokers wanted a way to cut through the bureaucracy and speed up the process. Independent credit reporting agencies, with their smaller, specialized staffs, began to fill the need.

Here's how it works. Your loan officer or broker collects proof from you that a mistake has been made, and he transmits that proof to the credit agency that provides the rapid rescoring service.

The rescorers, in turn, have special relationships with the credit bureaus that allow their requests to be processed quickly. The rescoring service sends proof of errors to special departments at the credit bureaus, and the departments contact the creditors (usually electronically). If the creditor agrees that an error was made, the bureaus quickly update your credit report. After that happens, a new credit score can be calculated.

The cost for this service is typically somewhere between $50 and $100 for each "trade line" or account that's corrected, although some agencies provide the rescoring for no extra charge, as part of a package of services provided to lending professionals.

The availability of rapid rescoring doesn't change the fact that you need to be proactive about your credit. Months before applying for any loan, you need to order copies of your reports and start challenging any inaccuracies. You also need to keep your correspondence about these errors. After all, rapid rescorers typically require some kind of paper trail to follow to prove to the bureau that the mistakes indeed exist.

But if you find yourself in the middle of getting a mortgage and an old problem recurs, rapid rescoring can help you get rid of the problem and save the deal.

So, how do you find one of these services?

If you're already dealing with a loan officer or mortgage broker, ask if she has access to a rapid rescoring service. If your lending pro has never heard of rapid rescoring—it's a recent enough innovation that some haven't—ask her to contact the agency that provides her company with credit reports to see if it's available.

Kyle, a mortgage consultant from Chicago, learned about rapid rescoring from an article I wrote and emailed me for suggestions on how to find such a service. It turned out that the agency that his company used for credit reports had long provided rescoring—Kyle just didn't know it.

If you're still in the market for a lending pro, make sure you inquire about access to rapid rescoring. Some of the online mortgage brokers, such as Quicken Loan, also use rapid rescorers to help their customers.

What if you're not in the market for a mortgage, or otherwise don't qualify for rapid rescoring, but you still want quick results?

You'll have to redefine your definition of "quick," for starters. Few things are rapid in credit repair. The following techniques typically won't show results in 72 hours, but you might see a noticeable bounce in your score in 30 to 60 days.

Boosting Your Score in 30–60 Days

Rebuilding your credit can be an agonizingly slow process, but there are a few shortcuts you can take that may increase your score in as little as a month or two. Among them:

Pay Off Your Credit Cards and Lines of Credit

One of the fastest ways to boost a score is to lower your *debt utilization ratio*—the difference between the amount of revolving credit that's available to you and the amount that you're using.

The best way to pay off revolving debt isn't with another loan, which would likely show up on your credit report anyway and could cause more damage. You're usually better off paying down the debt out of your current income, using cash that's sitting in a savings account, or selling stocks or other investments, as long as they aren't in a retirement account.

A riskier strategy might be to take out a 401(k) loan. These loans don't show up on your credit report, but you do face a big hazard: If you lose your job, you typically have to pay the money back quickly or you'll incur taxes and penalties on the balance. If you decide to take a 401(k) loan, make sure you'll be able to repay the loan quickly to minimize the risk.

Whatever you do, don't cash out a 401(k) or withdraw money from an IRA to pay off credit card debt. A few points' difference on your credit score is not worth the short- and long-term costs you'll pay for a premature withdrawal.

Use Your Credit Cards Extremely Lightly

Remember: The scoring formula likes to see a big gap between your balances and your limits—and it doesn't really care if you pay off your balances in full every month or carry them from month to month. What matters is how much of your credit limits you're actually using at any given time.

Some people insist they've boosted their scores by paying off their cards in full a few days before their statement closes. If their credit card issuers usually send out bills around the 25th, for example, these folks check their balances online about a week before and pay off whatever's owed, plus a few bucks to cover any charges that might crop up before the 25th. By the time the bills are actually printed, their balances are pretty close to zero. (If you use this technique, just make sure you make a second payment after your statement arrives if your balance isn't already zero. That will make sure you don't get dinged with late charges—and yes, that can happen, even though you made a payment earlier in the month.)

An easier way to keep your balances down is simply to pay cash for most purchases in the three months or so before you plan to get a loan.

Focus on Correcting the Big Mistakes on Your Credit Reports

If someone else's bankruptcy, collections, or charge-offs are showing up on your report, you will most likely benefit by having those removed. If an account you closed is reported as open, on the other hand, you'll probably want to leave it alone. Having an account reported as "closed" on your file can't help your score and might hurt it.

Don't ignore a collection just because it's small or it's listed as paid off. These are serious negative marks that can significantly depress a credit score. But don't get your knickers in a twist if the credit bureaus list the wrong employer or misspell your middle name. The credit scoring formula doesn't even consider these minutiae.

Use the Bureaus' Online Dispute Process

Some credit repair veterans swear they get quicker results this way, but you'll still need to make printouts of everything you send to the bureaus and every communication you receive from them.

See If You Can Get Your Creditors to Report or Update Positive Accounts

As you've read, not all creditors report to all three bureaus, and some don't report consistently. If you can get a creditor to report an account that's in good standing, though, you might see an immediate bump in your score.

Darren of New York had a great FICO score with Experian but only fair scores with Equifax and TransUnion. The reason? Most of his credit history was with a single credit union, and that credit union reported only to Experian.

> *"Since mortgage lenders [use] the middle score," Darren said, "I am not getting the best deal because that is not an accurate score."*

The middle score doesn't reflect Darren's full credit history.

Darren hasn't been able to convince his credit union to report to the other two bureaus. That means he's pretty much back to slow-lane solutions, such as getting a credit card or installment loan from a lender that reports to all three bureaus and making on-time payments.

What Typically Doesn't Work

There's a lot of folklore out there about how to fix a credit report fast. Most of it is bogus, such as what's outlined in the next sections.

Disputing Everything in Sight

Some of the phony credit repair places blitz credit bureaus with disputes about anything and everything. Because the disputed items are supposed to be temporarily removed from your file while the credit bureau investigates, the scam artists pretend they've actually purged your file.

Of course, most or all of the negative items simply come right back as soon as the original creditor confirms that they're correct. What might not come back are the accounts that are helping your score. The creditors might not bother to respond to the bureaus' requests for confirmation, and you could end up making matters worse.

Disputing too many items at once is also a good way to convince credit bureaus that you're filing "frivolous" disputes, and they might refuse to investigate at all.

To be on the safe side, don't dispute more than 3 or 4 negative items at once, unless (like Doug's bankruptcy accounts) your disputes are related. And don't pay anyone a fat fee to do this for you.

Creating a "New" Credit Identity

This is another favorite of scam artists. They might have you use a dead infant's Social Security number or tell you to apply for a taxpayer identification number, which the IRS typically issues to businesses.

Even if you do manage to pull off this fraud, you're left with an absolutely empty credit file. If you think it's hard to get loans when you have troubled credit, just try getting credit with no history at all. It could be years before you qualify for decent rates and terms, and by then all the negative marks you were so worried about would have either fallen off your original credit report or become so old that they would hardly affect your score.

Closing Troublesome Accounts

You can't get negative marks to fall off any quicker by closing accounts, and you might wind up seriously dinging your credit score.

Delinquencies, charge-offs, collections, and other negative marks can remain on your credit report for seven years, whether or not the original account is still open; bankruptcies can stay there for 10 years.

Even if you've had problems with an account, it might still be having a positive influence on your credit score. If it's one of your older accounts, it could be helping to make your credit history look nice and long—remember, older is better when it comes to credit scoring. If it's a revolving account, the credit limit is factored into your overall debt utilization ratio. If you close the account, you could make your existing balances look larger while making your credit history look younger than it is.

Paying Off Collection Accounts

As we covered in Chapter 7, paying off old debts can seriously hurt your score, because the payment can update the old account and make the negative look younger than it really is. This quirk in the credit scoring formula doesn't mean you shouldn't pay old debts—but you should negotiate hard with the collector to get the account dropped from your report as a condition of your payment.

9

INSURANCE AND YOUR
CREDIT SCORE

Tawny had been a loyal Allstate customer for 15 years. The Texas woman had paid her premiums on time and had never got a ticket, had an accident, or filed a claim.

Then her auto insurance premium tripled.

"I went through a devastating divorce where I lost my home and credit," said Tawny, who became a single mother with three small children. "About a year later, I got a notice from Allstate that my auto insurance rate was increasing . . . I wasn't too worried until I got my first bill. I went from paying $396 every six months to $1,200."

Kyra in Bridgeport, Connecticut never had trouble with her auto insurer. But when she tried applying for a renter's insurance policy with MetLife, she was denied.

"Although I have some previous credit problems, I would have never guessed in a million years that I would be denied a $200-per-year renter's insurance policy based on my credit history," Kyra steamed. "I'm self-employed, educated, and a productive citizen. I'm not any more likely to file an insurance claim than an unemployed individual with a high credit score."

Glen in El Paso got a notice that his auto premium was being raised to $125 a month, from $85. After getting the runaround from his insurer, he discovered the reason wasn't bad credit—it was too much credit.

"My wife had opened a GAP department store credit card with a $500 limit, and used it," Glen said. "Nothing more."

Glen was told that consumers who use more than half their available credit on a department store card "are considered high risk and therefore must pay higher rates."

John in Negley, Ohio, was recently notified that his homeowners' insurance premium would soar because of a recently filed bankruptcy. His only question for me: "Is this legal?"

That's typically one of the first questions many people have when informed that an insurer has raised their rates or denied them coverage based on their credit.

Here's the other question they understandably raise: What does my credit have to do with anything when it comes to insurance?

"My circumstances forced me into bankruptcy . . . I've never had an accident in my life," said Chestena in Texas, who was quoted auto rates of $400 to $2,000 more a year after her Chapter 7 filing. "Poor credit does not mean that you are a risk or that you are prone to accidents."

Insurers, though, think otherwise. They believe credit is an excellent predictor of whether you'll file a claim—better, in fact, than almost any other factor, including your previous driving history.

What's more, using credit for insurance decisions is not only legal in most states, it's the norm. The vast majority of big U.S. auto insurers—92 of the 100 largest companies—used credit information in 2001, according to a Conning & Co. survey, and so-called credit-based insurance scoring is widespread in the homeowners' market as well.

Credit scoring has been slower to take hold in Canada, but a study by the Insurance Bureau of Canada's Quebec office arm found an increasing number of companies employing credit information in their decisions, according to the Insurance Journal.

The way insurers use credit information, however, can differ markedly from the way lenders use the same data. That's why some people who have good credit scores and would qualify for the best rates and terms from most lenders still wind up paying higher premiums.

History of Using Credit Scores to Price Insurance Premiums

Insurers have actually been using credit information since at least 1970, when the Fair Credit Reporting Act first sanctioned the practice. Lamont Boyd, now a Fair Isaac executive, remembers his days reviewing credit reports as a young insurance underwriter in the 1970s.

Boyd says his job was to look for "clearly 'bad' signals," such as bankruptcies, foreclosures, or collections, which would be used as a reason to turn down the customer who was applying for insurance.

The process, according to Boyd and Fair Isaac, was subjective and inconsistent—much like the human-powered lending decisions being made in much of the credit industry at the time. People who might have been good risks, despite a few blemishes, were being turned down, whereas those who might have been worse risks were being accepted.

Fair Isaac decided to tackle the insurance market in the late 1980s, shortly after introducing the first credit scores based on credit bureau information. Although the company doesn't dominate insurance scoring the way that it does credit scoring, Fair Isaac has been instrumental in promoting the idea that credit information can give insurers an edge in predicting losses.

Fair Isaac introduced its first credit-based insurance score in 1991, and it hired actuarial consultants Tillinghast-Towers Perrin to review Fair Isaac's in-house studies of the links between credit history and insurance losses.

The correlations were so strong, said Tillinghast principle Wayne Holdredge, that the consultants were suspicious.

"We went back to the companies [that supplied the insurance data] and made them sign affidavits, saying that they hadn't cooked the books," Holdredge remembered. "Now the correlation is well understood, but back then it wasn't."

The cause of credit-based insurance scoring got another boost in 2000, when MetLife actuary James E. Monaghan published a study that matched 170,000 auto policies to the credit histories of the drivers.

Over and over, Monaghan found a correlation between black marks on credit reports and higher loss ratios for insurers. (A loss ratio measures how much an insurer pays out in claims for each dollar collected in premiums.)

Loss ratios rose steeply, for example, with the number of collection accounts appearing on a driver's record. Those who had no collection accounts cost the insurers an average of 74.1 cents for each dollar collected. Drivers who had one collection account had 97.5 cents in claims for each premium dollar collected, whereas those who had three or more collections cost insurers about $1.19.

Collection Accounts	Loss Ratio
None	74.1%
1	97.5%
2	108.4%
3 or more	118.6%

Monaghan found similar patterns with derogatory public records such as bankruptcies, liens, repossessions, and foreclosures . . .

Derogatory Public Records	Loss Ratio
None	73.8%
1	96.5%
2	104.2%
3 or more	114.1%

. . . with delinquencies . . .

Account Status	Loss Ratio
No lates	72.2%
At least one late	92.3%

. . . and with debt utilization, or how much of available credit was in use:

Leverage Ratio	Loss Ratio
1–10%	64.3%
11–39%	70.9%
40–60%	75.2%
61–80%	81.2%
80–100%	88.1%
101%+	96.6%

Correlations were a bit less linear for other credit information, such as inquiries, age of the consumer's oldest account, and amounts past due . . .

Amounts past Due	Loss Ratio
$0	70.20%
$100 to $199	95.9%
$200 to $499	92.7%
$500 to $999	107.2%
$1,000 to $2,000	97.2%
$2,000 to $5,000	100.5%
$5,000 to $10,000	106.1%
$10,000+	99.8%

. . . but the links were still strong enough to suggest a definite relationship between how well people handled their credit and how much they cost their insurers.

Monaghan's status as an industry insider, of course, led many consumer advocates to question his results. An independent study by the University of Texas at Austin a few years later, however, found similar patterns and a "statistically significant" link between credit scores and auto losses.

The UTA researchers matched credit scores to 153,326 auto policies issued in early 1998 and tracked which policies made claims in the ensuing 12 months.

"The lower a named insured's credit score, the higher the probability that the insured will incur losses on an automobile insurance policy," the UTA researchers said, "and the higher the expected loss on the policy."

The average loss per policy during the period was $695, but drivers who had the lowest credit scores cost their insurers $918, whereas those with the highest scores cost $558.

But What's the Connection?

What none of the studies have been able to prove is a *causal* link between credit and claims. In other words, they can't explain why poor credit should lead to more insurance losses.

Insurers speculate that people who are responsible with their credit might be more likely to be responsible with their cars and homes. Or, perhaps people who mismanage their finances are more likely to make claims because they need the cash.

MetLife's Monaghan, like others in the insurance industry, believes no one will ever be able to say for certain why the two are linked. He points out that it's impossible to prove a causal link for *most* factors used in insurance decisions.

The fact that you've been in an accident in the past, for example, doesn't *cause* you to have another accident. But most people can accept the idea that someone who has already had an accident or two might be more likely to have another one. It makes sense, in a way that using credit history for insurance does not.

The lack of a clear, logical link isn't the only thing that concerns consumer advocates about insurance scoring. Among the leading critics of insurance scoring is Birny Birnbaum, a former Texas insurance commissioner who believes insurance scoring might be illegally discriminating against low-income people and minorities.

Birnbaum doesn't believe the UTA study was rigorous enough to determine whether it's really credit, rather than some other factor, that correlates with insurer losses. He fears credit is actually some kind of proxy for a factor that insurers wouldn't otherwise be allowed to use, such as ethnic background or income.

As of this writing, though, the few studies that have been done on this issue have been either too small or too flawed to settle the issue either way.

Alaska regulators, for example, concluded that the use of insurance scoring is discriminated against rural, older, and low-income groups. But the Alaska study didn't use actual scores. Instead, the researchers took insurance industry designations that policyholders were "preferred," "standard" or "substandard" risks as a proxy for the policyholders' presumed credit risk. Insurers use plenty of factors besides credit to rate people, so the proxy probably wasn't a good one. The study also grouped its subjects by zip code, rather than examining individuals' histories of claims.

Another study by Washington state regulators seemed to show credit varied by ethnic background, but the researches admitted that the number of minorities polled was too small. The Washington study found that credit scores were lower among the poor, whereas one in Michigan found no racial bias but slightly higher scores among low-income groups.

A study in Maryland found credit scores were lower among minorities and low-income populations it studied, a finding that helped lead to serious restrictions on the use of credit information in that state. Even there, however, regulators said more research was needed.

The question may be settled relatively soon; the Fair and Accurate Credit Transactions Act (FACTA) of 2003 called for a comprehensive national study of the issue with results to be reported to Congress by December 2005. In the meantime, many states have adopted model legislation crafted by the National Conference of Insurance Legislators to regulate and restrict the use of credit. Among other things, the model legislation does the following:

- Forbids insurers from using credit information to deny, cancel, or fail to renew a policy

- Prevents insurers from using a consumer's lack of a credit history as a factor in determining premiums or coverage

- Requires insurers to review their credit-related decisions within 30 days if it turns out those decisions were based on erroneous credit reports.

Critics say the legislation does more to legitimize insurance scoring than protect consumers, but others say the laws at least provide insurers with some curbs.

Consumers already had some protections, theoretically, under the Fair Credit Reporting Act. The act requires insurers to notify consumers if credit information has affected a policy decision in any way, and include the following in the notification:

- The reasons for the insurer's decision

- The bureau from which the credit information was obtained

- Instructions on how the consumer can get a credit report

If my mailbag is any indication, some insurers aren't doing a very good job of following the law.

Glen, the man in El Paso whose insurance increased because of his wife's GAP card, played a long game of cat-and-mouse with his insurer when he asked why his rates had been hiked.

"My insurance agent passed me to corporate [headquarters]. Corporate threw up their hands and claimed it wasn't their fault, it's how [the company's score provider] scores my credit. I ask, how do they score it? They replied that I could only get this information from [the score provider]," Glen recounted in an email.

"[The score provider] won't answer the phone. You have to write in. I did. [The score provider's] answer was, 'It must be your credit report or your driving record.' I got both. Driving record perfect. Credit report even better than when I first got insurance.

"Finally [I] get a number to call. [The score provider said it] scores your credit according to how the insurance company wants them to. The insurance company then says they can't discuss the criteria [because] it's proprietary."

Glen said he finally pressured "someone at my insurance company to pressure someone at [the score provider] for an answer," which is when he learned that a maxed-out department store card was the culprit.

Clearly, it shouldn't be that hard to get answers.

Other readers have told me they called insurers for quotes, only to later find an inquiry by the insurance company on their credit reports. They say they weren't told a credit check would be run or given an explanation of how the information might affect their premium.

Even fans of insurance scoring admit that insurers sometimes fumble the ball. Boyd, Fair Isaac's point man on insurance scoring, agrees that many insurers aren't adequately explaining what they're doing. Customers are left baffled, as are the insurance agents who have the most contact with clients.

"The insurance companies have not done a good job educating their front-line agents to explain what's happening [to their customers],"
Boyd said.

Adding to the confusion is the lack of a dominant formula in the insurance scoring market. Fair Isaac sells its model to more than 300 insurers, but the biggest companies—State Farm, Allstate, Farmer's—have their own custom insurance scores using formulas they, and not Fair Isaac, developed.

Many people who have good credit scores, for example, have been told by their insurers that their rates increased because of their attempts to get credit.

If the insurer were using Fair Isaac's score, too many inquiries might at worst cause the customer to miss out on the insurer's best discounts, Boyd said. The consumer would still enjoy a break on premiums because of good credit, he said—it just might not be the best discount available.

If the insurer were raising everyone's rates by 15 percent, a customer who had a few too many inquiries might be charged 10 percent more, whereas the insurer's highest-rated customers might pay 5 percent more—and its worst-rated customers 20 percent more.

But Boyd couldn't vouch for how an insurer's custom score might treat inquiries, and the insurers who use custom scoring say such details are proprietary information.

Insurers are doing themselves no service by failing to explain the rules to their customers—particularly those who have good credit. As Boyd notes, someone who has bad credit might just accept a high premium as fate, but someone who has good credit is likely to react badly, even if they're just being shut out of the insurer's top tier of customers.

"Instead of getting an A, they got an A–," Boyd said, "and they're the ones who are going to start asking questions."

Insurers insist that credit-based scoring helps more people than it hurts. They say responsible policyholders pay less for their coverage than those who are more likely (in the insurers' view) to file a claim.

Indeed, some of the people who have written to me about their insurance scoring experience had happy news:

"I've been working hard on paying down debt and just bought a house this year," wrote Christopher of Lancaster, Pennsylvania. "About four months ago I got my new insurance premium bill in the mail and noticed that it was significantly cheaper then what I was paying before. Nothing had changed but my credit rating . . . . This was confirmed by my State Farm agent. [Insurance scoring] is a good thing."

What Goes into an Insurance Score

It's hard to be definitive about what does and doesn't affect your insurance score. Many big insurers have their own credit-based scoring models, and they're not talking much about how those work. Fair Isaac is talking some, but its formula doesn't dominate the insurance scoring world the way its credit score does the lending world.

But some information is better than nothing, and Fair Isaac is willing to share some of the details of what goes into its insurance scoring model. The factors used are similar to the ones considered with credit scoring, although their weight can vary:

- 40 percent of the average insurance score is determined by payment history—whether you've paid your bills on time. That compares to 35 percent for the credit-scoring model. As with credit scoring, the model looks at your payment history on different types of accounts, including credit cards and installment loans. Black marks such as delinquencies, charge-offs, collections, foreclosures, repossessions, liens, and judgments can seriously affect your score.

- 30 percent of your insurance score is based on your credit utilization, which is roughly the same percentage that your credit score uses. The score factors in the amount you owe on all of your accounts and how that compares to your credit limit (in the case of a credit card) or the amount you originally borrowed (for an installment loan).

- 15 percent of an insurance score has to do with the types of new credit you've been granted recently—how many new accounts you have, how long it's been since you opened a new account, and the number and type of inquiries on your report. By contrast, about 10 percent of the credit scoring model is derived from the number and types of new credit you've acquired.

- 10 percent of the insurance score is based on the length of time you've had credit—which counts for about 15 percent of your credit score. Both scores factor in the age of your oldest account as well as the average age of all your accounts.

- 5 percent of your insurance score measures types of credit in use, compared to 10 percent of your credit score. Once again, Fair Isaac is looking for that "healthy mix" of different types of credit, without providing much guidance about how many of each type of account you should have.

As you can see, Fair Isaac's insurance scoring model puts slightly more emphasis on your payment history and your recent behavior in applying for new credit. The age of accounts and their mix is slightly less important.

Keeping a Lid on Your Insurance Costs

The strategies you're learning in this book will help you improve and protect your credit, which should in turn help you to qualify for lower insurance rates in most states.

Good credit alone, however, isn't enough to keep you from overpaying for insurance. You need to be smart about the kinds of coverage you buy and how you use that coverage.

Whether your credit is good or bad, you should consider the steps outlined in the next sections to control your insurance costs.

Start Thinking Differently About Insurance

Lots of people feel somehow ripped off if they pay their premiums for years without ever making a claim. But this is exactly what you *want* to happen.

Insurance is meant to protect you against the kind of big expenses that could wipe you out financially—not to pay for the little stuff you could easily cover out of your own pocket.

So if you're using insurance properly and you never make a claim, that means you've never suffered a major catastrophe. Who among us wouldn't like to get through life without having a car totaled, a house burn down, or a lawsuit filed against us?

People who don't understand the role of insurance often try to shift as much risk as possible to their insurer—by choosing low deductibles, for example, or making claims for every little ding their cars suffer in supermarket parking lots. That's a quick road to higher premiums.

In fact, making lots of claims—or making even one of the wrong kind of claim, as you'll see later—can make it difficult for you to get coverage at all. Insurers share claims information and are on the lookout for people who are likely to cost them money. People who constantly turn to insurers to pay for damage they could have covered themselves often find fewer and fewer companies willing to insure them, and those companies are charging more and more to do so.

Does this seem unfair? If you think it does, you would expect to get some support from J. Robert Hunter, a consumer advocate and insurance expert for the Consumer Federation of America. He's been sharply critical of the insurance industry on many occasions, and he's seen by many reporters as the "go-to guy" when they need a succinct quote damning some bit of insurer foul play against consumers.

But Hunter, an insurance actuary and former Texas insurance commissioner, also knows how insurance is supposed to work. He maintains high deductibles on all his personal insurance policies, and he urges others to do so as well. He sets aside the money he saves on premiums to pay for out-of-pocket expenses.

Rather than protest, realize that this is how the insurance game is meant to be played. Preserve your coverage for the big disasters, and you'll save in the long run.

Raise Your Deductibles

This is one of the fastest and smartest ways to save money on insurance—but many people balk.

Raising your deductible means you'll pay less every year in premiums. You're also less likely to make claims for piddling stuff—claims that would likely result in your rates being jacked up.

So, if you can, boost your deductibles to at least $500 and preferably $1,000. Leave at least that much money in your savings account to cover the cost of any accidents, and you'll be money ahead in the long run.

Don't Make Certain Kinds Of Claims

There's something else that insurance is not—and that's a maintenance fund for your house and other property.

Insurance is designed to cover sudden and unexpected losses, such as a fire. If damage happens that you could have foreseen and prevented, you're on the hook. Insurers expect you to inspect, maintain, and protect your property without their help.

So, if a storm tears shingles off your roof and the resulting leak ruins your dining room ceiling, your policy will probably pay for repairs. If your roof is just old and falling apart, though, you'll have to reroof and replaster on your own dime.

Termite and rodent infestations are another frequent cause of damage that few insurers will cover. They figure you should have noticed the little critters and had them exterminated long before they had a chance to ravage your home.

If you make a claim for such problems, you very likely won't get a dime. But the claim could still count against you when it's time to renew your insurance.

Okay, let's say that the damage is indeed "sudden and unexpected": The rubber hose on your washing machine breaks and floods your house. Surely you should make *that* claim, right?

Maybe not. Insurers are particularly paranoid right now about water-damage claims. They've taken a beating from an exploding number of mold-related claims, including some famous ones, such as the contention from former *Tonight* show regular Ed McMahon that his home's toxic mold killed his dog.

Insurers share their claims experience in a huge database called C.L.U.E., for Comprehensive Loss Underwriters Exchange. Readers have told me that a single mention in the CLUE database is enough to blackball their home for years. Some say they didn't even make an actual claim, but simply asked their insurer for information.

Tami of Seattle asked a claims adjuster to evaluate what looked like damage to her bathroom floor. The adjuster determined that water splashing over the tub had seeped under the vinyl flooring sometime in the past, but that there was no current indication of moisture and the damage was entirely cosmetic.

"This was enough to have my house branded as 'water-damaged,'" Tami wrote. "When I tried to shop for a more reasonably priced homeowner's policy, I was told by my agent that it was impossible because no one is accepting new policies with a history of water damage. None of the six companies they represent would accept my house. I was also told that even if I entirely replaced the bathroom floor, it would have no effect on my policy status."

Oh, and it gets worse. A few readers have told me they had trouble selling their homes because of past water-related claims. Insurance companies balked at writing policies on the home for the new buyers; without insurance, mortgage lenders won't approve a loan.

Is this entirely rational? Of course not. Insurers are overreacting, as they tend to do. Eventually, a few insurance companies will realize they're avoiding some good customers, more will follow, and the water-related stigma will ease.

The best course for policyholders for right now, though, is prevention— and silence. Among the things you should be doing:

- Regularly inspect your home. Every few months, check your roof and foundation for leaks or standing water.

- Fix any leaks immediately.

- Replace hoses on older washing machines and dishwashers. Your plumber can point you to a type that's less likely to break.

- If you live in a cold climate, take steps to adequately insulate your pipes and prevent breakage.

If, despite your best efforts, you suffer water-related damage, seriously consider paying for repairs yourself if you possibly can, and avoid mentioning the incident to your insurer. Preventing the "water damage" stigma from attaching to your home could leave you money ahead in the long run.

Be a Defensive Driver

A patrol officer once explained to me that there are few true "accidents" on the road, but many, many crashes.

What's the difference? "Accident" implies the collision was out of the control of at least one of the drivers involved. That's rarely the case. Although one driver might be the direct cause, many times the other drivers could have avoided the crash had they been driving more defensively.

Obviously, there are exceptions. One of my dear friends was killed when a tractor-trailer rig flew over a center divider and smashed into his car. There's not much he could have done to avoid this accident other than staying home that particular day.

In most crashes, though, all of the drivers involved are at least partially at fault. If you've ever been hit, you can probably think of ways you could have avoided the collision. Maybe you were tailgating or driving too fast, not giving yourself enough time and road space to react. Or maybe you just weren't paying enough attention to what was going on ahead of you, or to the sides, or in your rear-view mirror. Who among us hasn't been distracted in a car by a child, a conversation, a cell phone, or a CD player?

Driving is dangerous business, and we owe it to ourselves, our passengers, and our pocketbooks to give it our full attention.

Use the Right Liability Limits

This might not save you money in the short run, but it could really save your bacon if you ever cause a serious accident or get sued.

Liability coverage pays for the damage you cause (or are accused of causing) to other people and other people's property. If someone slips and falls in your house or suffers serious injuries in a car crash for which you're found to be at fault, they can sue you for everything you're worth—and then some.

That's why you want to have liability coverage on your home and cars that's at least equal to your net worth. Some insurance experts recommend having twice that amount, or even more for people who are "lawsuit targets"—doctors, lawyers, public figures.

If you need to buy more coverage than your insurer offers—liability coverage for autos and homes usually maxes out at $500,000—consider buying a separate "umbrella" or personal liability policy. These policies kick in after the liability limits on your auto or homeowners insurance have been exhausted, and typically cost about $200 to $300 for $1 million of coverage.

Drop Collision and Comprehensive on Older Cars

Collision coverage pays for the damage you do to your own car in an accident, whereas comprehensive covers the other disasters that can happen—your car is stolen, dented in a hailstorm, or squashed by a falling tree branch.

This coverage is usually a good idea on newer cars, and is sometimes required by your financing company. The older your car, though, the less likely you are to get much money from the insurer even if the worst happens.

If your car is stolen or totaled, your insurance company will send you a check for an amount that's usually somewhere between its trade-in value at a dealership and what it would be worth if you sold it yourself.

If you haven't checked the value of your car lately, you might be surprised at how small that check is likely to be. (Online sites like Edmunds.com or KBB.com, the Kelley Blue Book site, can clue you in.)

If your car is old enough that you'd just replace it with a new one, and you wouldn't have much trouble coming up with a down payment on that next car without your insurer's help, then dropping comprehensive and collision is a no-brainer.

Shop Around

This has always been important, but never more so now that credit is such a factor.

Insurers tend to set their rates based on their own experiences. That's why premiums for the same drivers and cars can vary by thousands of dollars from one insurance company to the next, even when credit isn't a factor.

If your credit is mediocre or poor, you'll probably want to look for insurers that don't use credit information. There are still a number of these companies out there; they believe they've found other good ways to manage their risk.

You can look for an independent insurance agent who can tell you which companies don't use credit information, or simply call around and ask. But be advised that, unlike many other companies, an insurer can pull your credit without your permission. All it needs to have is your name and Social Security number. So, make sure the insurer doesn't use credit information before you give it identifying information.

If your credit is decent, you shouldn't shy away from companies that use insurance scores, because you could benefit.

A good place to start shopping is often your state Department of Insurance, which might offer some kind of premium survey that can help you see which companies are most likely to offer you a good deal, given your location and situation. (These regulators also might provide complaint surveys, so you can avoid the insurers that create the most problems for their customers.) An auto insurer that has a good track record of managing the risks of teenage drivers, for example, is likely to give you and your 16-year-old a better rate than one that wants to steer clear of underage drivers.

You can also use quote services such as InsWeb.com or call the companies directly.

You should be okay letting the insurers pull your credit at this point. Insurance inquiries shouldn't count against your insurance score. The Fair Isaac insurance score doesn't count insurance inquiries against you, but other insurance scores might.

Protect Your Score

Although insurance scores are a bigger mystery, much of the same behavior that protects your credit score should help improve and maintain your insurance score. Those behaviors include the following:

- Paying your bills on time

- Keeping balances low on credit cards and lines of credit

- Not applying for credit you don't need

If you do need to open new accounts, try to do so after you've renewed your policies for the year.

10

KEEPING YOUR SCORE HEALTHY

Mark from Seattle sent me a furious email after reading one of my columns about how to beef up a credit score.

Didn't I realize, he asked, that most of the strategies wouldn't work for someone who was out of a job, facing huge medical bills, and otherwise up to his ears in debt? How was he supposed to save his credit when he couldn't scrape together the cash to pay his rent?

Mark brings up a good point. All of the score-enhancing strategies in the world won't help if you can't pay your bills.

For Mark and millions like him, bankruptcy might be the only real option. It's a choice made by a huge number of people each year. A record 1.6 million consumer bankruptcies were filed in the U.S. in 2003. That's twice the number of 10 years earlier and nearly three times as many as filed in the entire decade of the 1950s.

Even then, far fewer households opt for bankruptcy than could actually benefit from filing, according to economist Michelle J. White, currently of University of California, San Diego.

Although less than 1 percent of households file each year, 15 percent have finances in such poor shape that they would be better off financially by going bankrupt, White estimated in 1998.

Many families simply don't have the resources to financially survive the inevitable setbacks that life throws them—job loss, divorce, accidents, or illness. And not all of these families are subsisting below the poverty line. Many have good incomes, nice homes, and new cars, but they've made no provision for the rainy days that come into everyone's lives.

In fact, the leading cause of bankruptcy is job loss combined with consumer debt and inadequate savings, according to comprehensive research by Jay L. Westbrook, Teresa A. Sullivan, and Elizabeth Warren, authors of *The Fragile Middle Class: Americans in Debt*. Medical bills, divorce, and burdensome mortgage debt are other key factors.

If you want to make sure you don't become yet another statistic, you can take measures to make sure that your score stays healthy. You might call them the three "do's" and four "don'ts" of bankruptcy-proofing your life.

The Do's of Credit Health

The following actions can help you survive life's setbacks and keep you out of bankruptcy court. The idea is to increase your financial flexibility and to protect yourself against some of the bigger risks you might face.

Pay Off Your Credit Card Balances

If one lesson about credit could be taught to every schoolchild, it should be this.

Paying off your credit cards every month is a good way to ensure that you'll always live within your means. You'll have the flexibility to weather bad times and take advantage of good times if you're not carrying a credit card balance around.

You won't be paying thousands of dollars—and more likely, tens of thousands of dollars—in unnecessary interest during your lifetime.

Consider this. Someone who carries a $5,000 credit card balance will pay somewhere around $70 a month in interest. If she were to invest that money instead, it could grow to nearly $250,000 over her working lifetime, assuming an 8 percent average annual return. That's a pretty big price to pay for the convenience of not paying cash.

Credit card debt also plays a big role in bankruptcies and other financial catastrophes. The actual crisis might be caused by job loss, divorce, or other setbacks, but it's their heavy burden of credit card debt that usually causes people to file.

Carrying a balance also leaves you vulnerable to the various games that credit card companies play, such as these:

- Deciding your fixed rate is no longer fixed, and raising it, or replacing your fixed rate with a variable one, or both.

- Raising your rate if you're late with a payment.

- Raising your rate if you charge too much.

- Raising your rate if you pay just the minimum.

- Raising your rate if you're late, maxed out, or having problems with any other creditor.

Michael in Westford, Vermont recently got a notice from his credit card company that his rate could soar to a stunning 29.99 percent if he was late with a single payment—to the issuing company or any other. Like most credit card companies, his issuer would periodically check Michael's credit reports and jack up his rates if any problems were detected.

"These new rules appear to be bait and switch tactics to me," Michael fumed. "[They] give you low rates and find a way to get you to the default rate."

The only winners in this game are the ones who don't play—who don't carry credit card balances from month to month and who never pay interest.

Despite what you might have heard, that's actually the norm in America.

Most American households have *no* credit card debt, according to the latest Federal Reserve study of consumer finances. About a quarter of American households have no credit cards and another 30 percent or so regularly pay off their balances. Most of those who do carry some credit card debt owe $2,000 or less.

That statistic you might have heard, that "the average American owes more than $9,000 in credit card debt," is bogus—even though the number is usually attributed to CardWeb.com, a legitimate research company that tracks credit card trends.

What CardWeb.com statistics actually show is that the average debt per American household with at least one credit card was $9,205 in 2003. To get that number, CardWeb simply divided the total outstanding credit card debt by the 84 million American households that it says have at least one credit card.

Using averages can be misleading, because a relative handful of consumers with huge credit card balances can skew the statistics.

It's kind of like measuring the "average" net worth of a group of 20 people when one of them is Warren Buffett. Even if the other 19 were stone cold broke, the "average" wealth of a person in that group would be more than $2 billion.

On a less extreme scale, that is what's happening with the CardWeb statistic. The Fed statistics show that fewer than 1 in 20 households actually owes more than $8,000, but the big balances by those few households are skewing the average.

If you're one of those who thought you were "average" in carrying credit card debt, realize you're not—and get ahead by leaving the debt behind.

Have an Emergency Fund

A whopping 43 percent of American households live paycheck-to-paycheck, with less than $1,000 in liquid assets. That's according to SMR Research, which has studied detailed income, asset, and debt statistics gathered by the Census Bureau.

Other researchers contend that only one in three American households has sufficient savings to weather even a short stretch of unemployment. Given how volatile the economy can be and the debt loads that many people carry, that's just begging for trouble.

Many people focus on the difficulty of scraping together enough cash to survive three to six months without a job. What these folks don't understand is that an emergency fund can be enormously freeing.

I was working for the *Anchorage Times* in Alaska when the venerable old paper announced one day that it was going out of business. We had less than 12 hours of notice. The announcement was made about 1 p.m., and the last edition rolled off the press around midnight.

People around me worried aloud about how they would pay their mortgages, their credit cards, and their child support. But when I went home and totaled the numbers, I realized I could live for six months on my savings without touching my retirement funds or altering my lifestyle all that much. If I made a few cutbacks, I could last a year.

The peace of mind I had that day, and in the month or so that it took to find my next reporting gig, is almost indescribable. Knowing that you can lose or walk away from any job is incredibly powerful.

You might think that you don't make enough money to set aside a reserve, but people who have studied the issue have found that whether you save has relatively little to do with what you bring in.

Steven Venti of Dartmouth and David Wise of Harvard used Social Security lifetime earnings and net income assessments for 3,992 households whose heads were near retirement age. Here's what they found:

- Savings and wealth vary enormously at every income level. Many low-income households don't have anything saved, but that's also true of many high-earning families.

- Disparities in wealth can't be explained by income alone, because some of the lowest-earning households managed to build significant wealth.

- Income differences explained just 5 percent of the variations, and life events—inheritances, big medical bills, divorce, the number of children—accounted for just 4 percent of the dispersion. Investment choices accounted for another 8 percent.

In other words, the vast majority of the differences in wealth had nothing to do with income, life events, or how the money was invested.

What did make the difference? How much the families chose to save. Venti and Wise determined that those who had a goal of saving built wealth, regardless of their circumstances.

Saving isn't easy, and if you're busy paying down credit card debt, it also might not be your first priority. But, as a starter, try to keep at least $1,000 in cash handy. Toss in any tax refunds you get, and as soon as possible set up an automatic transfer so that the money is whisked from your paycheck to your emergency fund before you even see it.

You'd be wise to keep the money somewhere safe and accessible, such as a savings account or a money market mutual fund. For a while in the go-go 1990s, it was fashionable to believe that people could put their emergency funds in the stock market and make great returns. The bear market that started in March 2000 pretty much squashed that theory. You don't want your fund to lose 50 percent or more of its value right when the economy is tanking and your boss decides that your job is now superfluous.

If you're a homeowner, consider opening a home equity line of credit as a stand-in for an emergency fund until you can get the appropriate amount saved. For this strategy to work, though, you have to leave the line unused. Don't be tempted to rack up more debt by this relatively cheap form of borrowing.

Have Adequate Insurance

This is much easier said than done, of course. Health insurance can be expensive and, for many people, tough to get. That's why more than 40 million Americans are uninsured, and why medical bills are a factor in about one out of five personal bankruptcies in the U.S., according to studies by VISA and other researchers. Medical bills are the direct cause of at least one in 10 filings, according to research by Harvard professor Elizabeth Warren.

Medical bills are a negligible factor in Canada, which has universal health insurance. It's one of the reasons why Canada's bankruptcy rate is less than one-third that of the U.S.

Even people who have health insurance are often blindsided by huge medical bills. Alana's policy required her to make 30 percent co-payments—which was affordable when the Indianapolis woman sought routine care, but not when her daughter was born critically ill.

"My daughter . . . spent several weeks in intensive care. Add this to already maxed out credit cards," Alana said, "and it was a recipe for disaster."

Alana wound up filing bankruptcy to wipe out thousands of dollars in doctor and hospital bills.

Some people who are young and healthy think they don't need coverage, but no one can predict when an accident or major illness might strike. If you have coverage through your employer, by all means take advantage of it. If you don't and your income is low, check to see if your state offers bare-bones coverage.

Another solution: a high-deductible or "catastrophic" policy, perhaps combined with a health savings account. You're required to pay the first $1,000 or more of medical expenses before your coverage kicks in, but your out-of-pocket expenses are capped in the case of accident or major illness. High-deductible policies tend to cost 25 percent to 50 percent less than a full-coverage HMO policy, depending on how much you're willing to pay out of pocket.

If you buy a policy that's compatible with the new health savings accounts, you can put an amount equal to your deductible into an HSA and write the contribution off on your taxes. You can withdraw the money for medical expenses at any time, tax free; any money you don't use can roll over tax-deferred from year to year. You can find out more about HSAs at www.hsainsider.com, or by talking to a knowledgeable insurance agent.

Take a look, too, at your liability coverage. This is the part of your home-owners and auto insurance that protects you against lawsuits. Make sure your liability limits on each of your policies is at least equal your total net worth.

I'd like to include a pitch for disability insurance, as well, if it's available through your employer. You're much more likely to be disabled and unable to work than you are to die before you retire, yet most people don't have a long-term disability plan. You can also try buying an individual policy, although these have become rather expensive in recent years.

The Don'ts of Credit Health

Building and protecting your financial resources is a good start, but equally important is limiting how much debt you incur in your lifetime.

Don't Buy More House Than You Can Afford

It seems that everybody who is involved in the home-buying process is pushing you to buy the most house you possibly can. Your friends and relatives might be urging you to stretch, and your real estate agent might have her eye on the bigger commission that a more expensive house can bring.

Lenders have greatly loosened their standards and will give you more money than you can comfortably afford to repay. Mortgage payments used to be capped at 26–28 percent of your gross monthly income, but many lenders today let homebuyers borrow up to 33 percent, and some go even higher, to a whopping 50 percent or more of their gross.

Lenders know you probably will do whatever it takes to keep your home, even if it means short-changing your retirement, giving up vacations, and driving yourself deep into debt. Homeowners' desire to hang on to their houses despite "insurmountable debt," according to researchers Sullivan, Warren, and Westbrook, is a leading contributor in Chapter 13 bankruptcies.

Many homebuyers also underestimate all of the ancillary costs of buying a home, such as maintenance, repairs, improvements, and decoration. At the same time, lenders are falling over themselves to extend you credit, because homeowners are generally viewed as more stable and financially responsible than renters.

Lillian and her now ex-husband were actually conservative when they bought their first home, keeping their mortgage payments to just 20 percent of their gross income. The problems started immediately, though, as lenders rushed to give them money.

"It was heady to have so many offers of loans after we purchased our home," Lillian wrote. "We soon found ourselves borrowing to buy carpeting, insulation, storm windows, landscaping, and even a new pick-up truck.

"Within three years, we were insolvent," Lillian continued. "Then the worst happened . . . My husband lost his job, and our insolvency was more than inconvenient, it was critical."

In reality, nobody else—not your lender, your real estate agent, or your relatives—can tell you how much house you can really handle. That depends on a number of factors that others typically don't know, such as how much you need to save for retirement, how many children you want to have, and how tied down to a house you want to be.

Buying a house today is a lot different than it was 20 or 30 years ago, when your parents might have bought their first house. Back then, rampant inflation meant big annual pay raises, which made a mortgage payment look smaller and smaller as years passed. People back then were also more likely to be covered by a traditional pension, which meant they didn't have to save gobs of money to pay for their own retirements. And fewer families had two wage-earners, which meant Mom could always go to work if Dad lost his job. Today, many families need both salaries to pay the mortgage, and the loss of one is a disaster.

Those are among the reasons why it's often smart to limit your total housing payments—principle, interest, taxes, and insurance—to 25 percent of your gross monthly income. You might be able to go a bit higher if you have no other debt or a great pension that lessens your need to contribute to your own retirement. You might want to aim a little lower if you plan to have kids and want one spouse to stay home to care for them.

Don't Overdose on Student Loan Debt

Student loans are often referred to as a "good" debt—the kind of borrowing that will increase your earning power and thus more than pay for itself.

Unfortunately, lots of students are taking a good thing way too far.

Michelle of Indiana emailed to say she owed $120,000 in student loans—and was making just under $50,000 as an assistant professor in her field. She had consolidated all of her federal loans and deferred payment when she could, but the cold hard truth was setting in.

"I am staring at a debt that I cannot repay. Our salaries have been frozen for the next two years due to state budget problems, and I've calculated that even paying the minimum on all my loans would leave me with less than 100 dollars to live out the month. Is bankruptcy my only option? I'm not seeing a way out of this."

I had to give her some news that was even worse than she was expecting. Student loans can almost never be wiped out in bankruptcy court. Federal law requires that student borrowers prove repayment would be an extreme hardship—a tough standard to meet "unless you're totally permanently disabled," in the words of Los Angeles bankruptcy attorney Leon Bayer.

You'll do yourself a huge favor by limiting how much you borrow. Your student loan payments shouldn't total more than 10 percent of your first job's monthly pay. Although how much that lets you borrow depends on the interest rates you'll pay, you can pretty much figure that your total student loan debt shouldn't equal more than one-half to two-thirds of that first job's annual pay.

What if you discover that you're already in too deep? If you haven't gotten your degree yet, you can save yourself some pain by transferring to a less expensive school or taking a year off to work. If you're already out, you should consider consolidating your federal loans to stretch out the payments. You might even need to work a second job for a while to raise the cash to retire this debt.

Don't Raid Your Retirement or Your Home Equity to Pay Off Credit Cards

Lenders love to push home equity loans or lines of credit as the "solution" to your debt problems. In fact, these loans often cause more problems than they solve:

- You're draining away the equity that could give you a financial cushion in an emergency. Especially if your savings are meager, you might need to turn to your home equity to help you survive a job loss. How are you going to feel if your equity is already gone?

- More importantly, you're not dealing with the overspending that got you into credit card debt in the first place. Nearly two-thirds of the people who took out home equity loans between 1996 and 1998 to pay off credit cards had incurred more card debt within two years, according to a study by Atlanta research firm Brittain Associates.

- You're turning unsecured debt, which could be erased in bankruptcy, into debt that's secured by your home. If you can't pay this loan, you could lose your house.

Turning to your retirement funds isn't much better, as I detailed in Chapter 5, "Coping with a Credit Crisis." The taxes and penalties that are due on premature withdrawals will equal up to half of any money you take out. You'll also be missing out on the future tax-deferred returns that money could have made; you should figure that every $10,000 withdrawal costs you at least $100,000 in future retirement income.

Even loans against 401(k)s are risky, because you typically have to pay the money back promptly if you lose your job, or the balance will be taxed and penalized as a withdrawal.

A much better course, for most people, is to pay off credit card debt out of current incomes whenever possible. Leave retirement funds for retirement and your home equity for true emergencies.

Credit and Divorce: How Your Ex Can Kill Your Score

Even if you're doing everything right with your own finances, you can still take the fall for someone else's mistakes. Albert, an Army officer, remarried after his divorce 10 years ago. However, his ex-wife's sloppy credit habits are still trashing his credit score.

"The problem is that she was not ordered to refinance the house in her name only," Albert wrote. "Since then, she has never made the mortgage payments on time, and it reflects on my credit report. Except for that pay-ment, my present wife and I have perfect credit."

It's not that his ex can't afford the $263 monthly payment, Albert explained; both she and her second husband have good salaries. She's just habitually late.

Albert contacted the lender and the credit bureaus, all of which gave him the same answer: As long as his name is still on the loan, the payments will continue to show up on his report and affect his credit score.

Many divorced people are shocked to discover that their exes can hurt their credit years after the split is final. Even when a divorce decree clearly spells out that the former spouse is responsible for paying a debt, you can still be on the hook.

That's because creditors don't have to care what a divorce decree says. You made your agreements with lenders well before your divorce, and your lenders didn't have any say in the decree's terms. So if your name is still on the loan, the account was opened jointly, or your spouse was added as an authorized user of a credit card, you can be held responsible.

Some people are in this fix because they didn't use an attorney to help with their divorces, but some did have legal representation—and still weren't alerted to the potential problem.

Many lawyers let couples work out how they're going to handle joint debts on their own, said attorney and financial planner Amy Boohaker of Sarasota, Fla. The attorney might not know, or bother to communicate, the potential ramifications of not shutting down joint credit.

As a result, I regularly get anguished emails from people whose credit report is littered with an ex's delinquencies, charge-offs, collections, and even bankruptcies.

The best time to handle the issue is well before the divorce is final, but there are some things you can do even afterward. Read on.

Get Your Credit Reports

Identify every credit account that your ex could access. If the account is listed as joint, rather than individual, your spouse can probably use it. If the account is listed as individual and is still open, call the creditor to find out whether your spouse is listed as an authorized user.

Take Action

You might be able to get your spouse removed as an authorized user with a phone call to the card issuer, but follow up in writing.

With joint accounts, your best bet is to close them whenever possible, although you might have to settle for "freezing" the account if you owe a balance. A freeze is supposed to prevent either of you from using the card.

Unfortunately, though, sometimes a spouse can talk a creditor into lifting a freeze, which is why it's important to put your request in writing, note that you and your spouse are divorcing, and make it clear that you won't be responsible for any charges made after the freeze is in place.

If you do have a balance, it should be transferred as soon as possible to the card of the spouse who will be responsible for paying it off.

What if your spouse can't get credit in his or her own name? If the divorce isn't final, you might want to take on the debts and get a larger property settlement to offset the extra burden, rather than leave your future credit score in the hands of someone who could so easily trash it.

If the divorce is final, you might need to take over the payments to prevent further damage to your credit rating. Your divorce decree might allow you to take your ex back to court for reimbursement, but either way, you shouldn't leave your credit in his or her hands for a second longer.

A few months after you make your requests, get another copy of your credit reports to make sure the accounts are listed properly. If an account that was closed is listed as open, or if the balance on a frozen account has grown, follow up immediately with the creditor.

Don't Be Late

Divorce negotiations can drag on almost endlessly, but just one late payment can really hurt your credit. You might need to make a few payments on debts that will ultimately be your spouse's, just to make sure they don't go delinquent while you're still responsible for the account.

Dealing with Mortgages, Car Loans, and Other Secured Debt

Ideally, you should either sell the asset and split up the proceeds, or refinance the loan so that you're no longer on the hook. If refinancing is an option, make sure it gets done before the divorce is final.

Sometimes, though, your ex won't want to sell and won't have the income or credit to swing a refinance. If that's the case, set some kind of time limit on how long you're willing to stay on the loan.

If your ex wants to continue living in the family home with your kids, you might agree that the house will be sold when the youngest is 18. Make sure this agreement is part of your divorce decree, and ask the lender to send loan statements and payment coupons to you so that you can make sure the loan is getting paid. At the very least, you should be able to get Internet or phone access to the account so that you can monitor the situation.

If you're already divorced, you might still want to get access to the account and make the payments if your ex is falling behind. Again, your divorce decree might allow you to take him or her back to court for reimbursement.

If your ex could refinance but won't, you might have to resort to bribes—a cash payment or more time with the kids in exchange for getting a new loan.

Whatever your arrangement, don't sign a quit-claim or let your name be taken off the title as long as your name is still on the loan. You don't want to be responsible for the debt if you no longer own the asset.

Consider a Fraud Alert

If you're in a particularly nasty divorce, or if your spouse is unethical, you might wind up a victim of identity theft. After all, your spouse knows your Social Security number, your address, and just about any other detail required to open up a new account in your name, run up a balance, and leave you holding the bag.

Your ex could even file a bankruptcy in your name, because many districts don't require identification when a bankruptcy is first filed. By the time the first hearing rolls around, the bankruptcy has already been logged in the huge central database combed by credit bureaus and will show up on your credit report. Such a bogus filing is a crime, but that doesn't prevent some vengeful exes from doing it.

Asking the three credit bureaus to put a fraud alert on your files won't necessarily prevent any of this from happening—particularly not the bankruptcy filing. But it should make it a little harder for your ex to open new accounts in your name. You should get regular copies of your credit reports—at least twice a year—to monitor for anything suspicious.

If a phony bankruptcy has been filed, you'll need to hire a bankruptcy attorney who knows how to get the filing expunged.

Look for Lenders Who Aren't FICO-driven

Although the vast majority of mortgage companies use FICO scores in their lending decisions, a few don't—and that can benefit someone whose ex is creating problems.

Albert, for example, wants to buy another home after the Army transfers him to a new station. Even if he succeeds in getting his ex to refinance the loan, his credit score will still be affected by all the late payments.

Albert could benefit from a lender that doesn't sell its loans to investors like Fannie Mae and Freddie Mac that require the use of FICO scores. If the lender keeps its loans in house, rather than selling them on the secondary market, it's often more flexible with its lending standards.

Albert's best bet might be to find an experienced mortgage broker who can evaluate your situation and get you in touch with a lender that can base its decision on your behavior, rather than your ex's.

In Conclusion: The Three-year Solution

There's one more issue to address that can have a profound effect on your credit score, your finances and your life. And that's the issue of how much you can "afford" to borrow on something other than a house or an education.

Many people assume they can afford something if they can make the monthly payments. But that kind of short-term thinking will shackle you to a lifetime of paying interest on stuff that will break, wear out and become useless long before the last payment is due.

Either that, or you'll trap yourself into an "upside down" loan.

That's the case for about 80 percent new car buyers, who drive off the lot owing more on their cars than the vehicles are worth. Many come into dealerships still owing money on their trade-ins, and they compound the problem by taking out five-, six- or even seven-year loans. Those longer payback periods, combined with the speed in which a new car depreciates, means they'll stay upside down for years.

The problem? Your car gets totaled, or you lose your job, and you can't get enough for your car to pay off the loan. You'll still owe thousands, and you might be wheel-less besides.

One way to avoid that problem entirely is, of course, to pay cash for everything. This approach has plenty of advocates, and if you understand the power of compound interest, you can see why.

Let's say Ralph decides to buy a car and finance it with a $20,000 loan. At 5 percent interest over five years, Ralph will make 60 payments of $377.42, for a total cost of $22,645.

Jamal, by contrast, decides to save up to buy a car. He invests $294.09 a month for five years at 5 percent interest and ends up with $20,000 cash— but only contributed $17,645 out of his own pocket. The rest of the money came from interest paid on his savings.

The difference between the two approaches is substantial: Ralph will pay nearly $5,000 more than Jamal.

Many people, though, lack Jamal's discipline. There are so many other demands on their money—and so many tempting things to buy—that the cash never quite gets from their paychecks to the savings accounts.

I hope that as you gain more control over your credit and your finances, you'll become the kind of savvy consumer who can pay cash for a car and other consumer purchases. In the meantime, though, you can save yourself a ton of money and potential hassles with the three-year rule.

By that, I mean not borrowing any amount of money—other than a mortgage or a student loan—that you can't pay back in three years.

A three-year loan means you'll face bigger payments, but you'll pay far less interest now and over your lifetime. You'll also reduce the time you spend "upside down" on your purchase, even if you can't make much of a down payment.

You should consider this approach for many home improvements as well. Most of the stuff people do to their homes, from remodeling kitchens to adding swimming pools, doesn't add as much value to their houses as the project costs. In other words, the improvements aren't an investment— they're consumption.

Give yourself a three-year payback period, and you'll rein in some of the temptation to overspend. You don't have to go without—you just have to get realistic about costs.

What's the payoff for all of this hard work, discipline and restraint? Greater wealth, greater freedom and a greater ability to get the loans you need, when you need them, at the best possible rates.

Instead of being at lenders' mercy, you'll be the one in charge.

And wasn't that the whole reason for reading this book in the first place? Instead of being turned down for credit, or paying too much for it, you've learned the best ways to fix, improve and protect your score so you can qualify for the best rates and terms. You've learned to separate fact from fiction when it comes to credit scoring, and discovered the fastest ways to rebuild after a financial disaster.

You've realized that you don't have to feel helpless or outgunned by creditors. By learning how credit and credit scoring really work, you've taken back the power to manage your finances. May that knowledge help you build the life you really want.

INDEX